ON THE ROAD TO FROG EYE

A FAMILY HISTORY

JOYCE MATTHEWS MCQUEEN

Published by High Tide Publications, Inc.
www.hightidepublications.com
j.johansen@hightidepublications.com

Thank you for purchasing an authorized edition of *On the Road to Frog Eye.*

High Tide's mission is to find, encourage, promote, and publish the work of authors. We are a small, woman-owned enterprise that is dedicated to the author over 50. When you buy an authorized copy, you help us to bring their work to you.

When you honor copyright law by not reproducing or scanning any part (in any form) without our written permission, you enable us to support authors, publish their work, and bring it to you to enjoy.

We thank you for supporting our authors.

On the front cover: Phyllis, Wayne and Joyce Matthews
On the back cover:
Top Row: Margaret Cline Jones Matthews; Joyce Matthews McQueen
Second Row: Wayne Lake Matthews, Phyllis Cline Matthews, Glen Ingram Matthews
Third Row: Lake and Margaret Matthews

Edited by Cindy L. Freeman   www.cindylfreeman.com
Book Design by Firebellied Frog   www.firebelliedfrog.com

THIS BOOK IS DEDICATED

TO MY FAMILY.

IMPERFECT?

YES!

LOVED IN SPITE OF IT?

ALWAYS!

MEMAW

CONTENTS

On The Road To Frog Eye

Part One

INTRODUCTION

This is the story of our family as I remember it with a few tidbits from my siblings. For one reason or another, neither of them can remember squat, or so they claim. Since both of our parents— Lake S. Matthews who died on April 11, 1987 and our beloved mother, Margaret Cline Jones Matthews who died August 18, 2005—are no longer around to help me out here, I am on my own. With what few notes I have taken along the way, and a great memory—to date anyway—it has taken a while to piece together this story. No doubt, the gift of a great memory is inherited from the Matthews side of the family.

The stories are as factual as any that have ever been written, and then there are the ones that were dropped in my lap by Dad's family. Family being his Aunt Agnes Hoffman (our paternal grandmother, Amy's sister) and by Daddy's sisters, Josephine

My paternal aunt - Josephine Mahalia Matthews - Age 13 months
Taken at the home of Aunt Agnes Hoffman, Chrisfield, MD*

Mahalia Matthews and Mary Jo Matthews. Many stories were not shared by our parents or grandparents, as that is the way it was. Those tales were swept under the rug in hopes they would be forgotten. Then there is *my* account that was swept under the rug also, out of fear.

The roads on a long journey always get a little bumpy, and *The Road to Frog Eye* is no exception. So, buckle up and enjoy the laughs, the tears, and the mud holes along the way, as that is exactly what they were: mud holes. Sometimes the wagons rolled right through them and other times the wagon wheels sank deep, and there was no pathway to salvation for the wagon or its driver.

The kids involved include my siblings Wayne Lake, Phyllis Cline, and Glen Ingram Matthews. It touches on the childhood of our father, his sister Josephine, and his half-siblings Mary Jo and Allen Matthews, as well as others who played a part in our lives every day.

The family continues to grow, and, as of today, Mother and Daddy have thirty-five living descendants. Hopefully, there will be many more healthy beautiful babies that live long lives. Dad's sister Josephine (Josie) passed away on December 26, 2015 in Delaware at the age of ninety-two. Mary Jo lives with her son Glen in Nevada, and her brother Allen still lives with his wife and daughter on a parcel of the Matthews farm. A small parcel of the land that was purchased 121 years ago in Marumsco, Maryland by our great-grandfather George Alfred Matthews and great-grandmother Josephine Darby Matthews.

Allen and Glen Matthews 1959

Wayne Matthews 1959

Phyllis and Glen Matthews
Taken in the driveway on Corn Stock Road
Marion, MD - 1957

COUNTRY KIDS

The majority of my memories are from that place we called home in Marumsco, Maryland on the *Road to Frog Eye*. In April 1960, Mother, Dad, and my three younger siblings moved to Syringa, Virginia. Wayne had just turned eleven, Phyllis was eight, and Glen was seven when they settled on this side of the Chesapeake Bay.

We were born and raised in the country, and country kids we were indeed. Dad and Aunt Josie were both born at the Matthews farm on *The Road to Frog Eye*, as Mary Jo and I were. Wayne, Phyllis, Glen, and Allen were all born in the hospital in Salisbury, Maryland.

That road was where little kids with freckles and sun-bleached hair lived, laughed, and played every day. We all ran bare footed through the cornfields, rode on top of hay wagons, and played in the irrigation ditches with our friends. No doubt, our guardian angels sat on our shoulders, as we somehow made it back home every evening filthy, tired, and hungry.

When I was a baby, my days were spent on Hudson Street in Crisfield, Maryland. A woman by the name of Mamie Lewis lived across the street from Aunt Agnes, and I was told she was my babysitter. I have a photo of her holding me at that time. If I wasn't with her, I was at my Mom-Mom Amy and Mom's house. Our parents had rented a small house on Pear Street in Crisfield before I was born but had moved to Marumsco just before then—more than likely when Dad's grandfather George died in June 1943. They both were working at Briddells in Crisfield during WWII, so the puzzle pieces come together.

They had lived in Crisfield only a short time and Mother went to the Church of God, a Pentecostal church with Mom-Mom Amy one Sunday morning. Mother said every time the preacher opened his mouth the congregation would hold up their arms while shaking them and holler "Amen." She said it got louder and louder until it reached a point that you could no longer hear the preacher. Then they started speaking in some kind of language she did not understand. One time, the woman in the pew in front of Mother was carrying on so much that she passed out on the floor and her dress went up around her waist. A couple of other women hurried to adjust her dress to cover her underwear and the preacher shouted, "Do not touch her. She is feeling the spirit of the Holy Ghost." So they left her lying there. Mother had never witnessed a church sermon like it before and kept thinking, *just let this be over and get me out of here.* It was too much for her to digest, and she never attended the church again.

Daddy would take me down on Main Street in Crisfield, and he was always stopping to talk to everyone. As we walked away, he would say, "That was your cousin," and I did not understand what he was telling me. One day he took me to the old train station that someone had turned into an eatery, and there he stopped to talk to a man in a brown uniform. The man wanted to buy me an ice cream cone, and it took me a long time to pick out a flavor from all the tubs in the case. I settled on a rainbow ice cream cone with lots of colors. That was the first ice cream cone that I had ever tasted, or at least the first one I remember. I was to learn later that the man was Mom-Mom Amy and Aunt Agnes' brother, Wells Marshall, who was Dad's uncle of course. Once I was old enough to learn how large the Marshall family was, I understood why every other person that Daddy spoke to was a cousin. I am still in contact with several of the Marshall cousins, including Daddy's first cousin Bobby Marshall, the last one living from that generation.

DADDY HAD STORIES TO TELL

Daddy had stories that he told us regarding how all four of us children came to live with him and Mother. The stories went as follows:

Joyce...Dr. George Coulbourne was running across the field with his black satchel in hand and had to cross the hog pen to get to the house. He lost his footing in the mud, fell, and the satchel flew open. Inside there were two babies. The hogs ate one baby, and the turd, being me, lived.

Wayne...The turkey buzzards laid a nest of eggs, and they all hatched with baby buzzards except one. That egg busted open, and there was Wayne. Mom and Dad rescued him from the buzzard's nest.

Phyllis....She was sitting on top of a rainbow when someone greased her butt, and gave her a push. She slid down the rainbow and Mom and Dad caught her at the bottom. (How sweet!)

Glen...He was found in the cabbage patch under a huge cabbage leaf, and there may have been a rabbit in play somewhere.

If you think words do not affect a child's mind, think again. I have no clue how many years I envisioned this doctor in black pants and hat running across that field, jumping over fences with that little black bag and the horrible scene of a hog eating a baby. I could even envision Phyllis sliding down that rainbow and Mom and Dad swooping her up. But just as scary as the hogs eating the baby was his story regarding the buzzards. There were a lot of them on the Eastern Shore, and they were always flying overhead. I kept an eye on those suckers making sure they didn't swoop down to get me.

Then there were the serious stories that were instilled in our minds, the stories that you never forgot, like when Daddy spoke of how he had gotten two horrible beatings with a leather strap by his father Grover Matthews when he was a child.

Daddy attended the small two-room school in Marumsco for elementary school, and there was an outhouse at the school. There had been a heavy snowstorm earlier but they had still class that day. As they watched the female teacher go to the outhouse, he and several other boys decided to play a prank on her. They pushed the outhouse over with the door lying face down on the ground. Well, it must have been easier to push over than it was to set back up. There is no question that the boys deserved to be punished, and Daddy was, of course. He said that was the first time his father beat him hard with a leather strap.

Then there was the story about Charlie Smith (you will learn who he was later). Charlie was out working the farm with a horse and plow on a hot summer day. Pop-Pop Grover gave Daddy a quart jar of ice tea to take out to Charlie, and Daddy started across the field with the tea. Daddy was barefoot, and it wasn't long before the hard clumps of sun-baked soil were hurting his feet. He poured the tea on the ground and ran back home. When Pop-Pop asked him if he gave Charlie the tea, he answered, "Yes sir." That evening when Charlie came to the house, Pop-Pop went out to meet him and asked if he enjoyed the tea. Charlie said, "I ain't seen no ice tea." Pop-Pop Grover beat Daddy so bad with a leather strap for lying that he had to stand and eat off the mantle for a week.

When we were kids and did something wrong, Daddy would threaten with, "I ought to give you a beating like my father gave me...one that you will never forget." I would get concerned and scared when he threatened with a leather strap, and I didn't ponder how bad it might hurt, but wondered many times where I would stand to eat. We did not have a mantle in our house.

WHERE WE LIVED

We lived on the Eastern Shore of Maryland in the County of Somerset. I am sure the main post office was listed as Marion Station by that time, but we actually lived closer to a place called Marumsco on the Road to Frog Eye Church. The Marumsco post office was inside the huge old wooden general store, and one of my best friend's mothers, Lillian Adams, was the postmaster and store clerk. As a matter of fact, the school bus went to that store every morning, turned around, and came back up the road. The last time I visited, I was shocked to see a green-and-white sign standing on the corner of the highway that read "Cornstalk Road." I do not remember there being a road name when I was a child, but Mary Jo claims it has always had that name. I must dispute her claim, and, in fact, some of the old census records list the homes "On the Road to Frog Eye Church," with no mention of Cornstalk Road, so that name must have come along later. The old deeds identify it as Marumsco Road. Ron Adams believes it was given the official name of "Cornstalk Road" when the 911 emergency system was put in place, which would make sense.

Our house had two rooms upstairs and two rooms down and had been built by our grandfather Grover Matthews on the back of his property near the woods. I was born in that house in 1943 on the same land where Daddy, Aunt Josie, and Mary Jo were born. Sometime before Wayne was born five years later, the house was moved out on the road, on an angle of our grandfather's home that sat up a lane. I do not remember the house being moved across the field. It was a basic two-story modest home in that day without running water, not a big old sprawling farmhouse.

A path was created on the back of our yard that ran down the field along a ditch line then across the ditch over a plank and over to Pop-Pop's field where the path continued, past the outhouse. Somewhere along the journey, our grandfather had a new four-holer outhouse built that straddled the ditch. To this day, I do not understand why a toilet would be a four-seater, unless going to the outhouse was a family event. Mary Jo and I spent a lot of time in that outhouse together, as well as the older one that it replaced.

The first thing you did upon entering the outhouse was to look into dark hole to make sure no snakes would rear up and bite your arse. Of course, it was so dark in the hole-to-nowhere, you would never have seen one lurking there.

Once you were confident that all was clear and got comfortable on the seat, you thumbed through each page of the Montgomery Ward or Sears catalog that had been placed there. I assure you there was never a roll of toilet paper in that outhouse. Mary Jo and I spent hours looking at all the pretty clothes and shoes in the catalog, but the big payoff came when the Christmas catalog was finally discarded to the outhouse. It was then that you could dream about the toys you wanted, hoping Santa would bring them for Christmas. I still remember the sinking feeling as I stripped the pages of the Christmas catalog, and eventually, it too became a thing of the past.

No doubt that new toilet became a shield from the cold winds when we were outside playing. I do remember seeing a bucket, basket, or something filled with corncobs sitting in the corner of that toilet. I can only guess they had Pop-Pop Grover's name on them or perhaps Charlie Smith's.

I always hated walking the plank across the ditch to get to Pop-Pop Grover's house as I feared the snakes that might be there, but I do not recall ever seeing one. It is possible that snakes did not have a chance on that land due to all the hunting dogs and Pop-Pop's flock of Guinea hens. The hens served as watch dogs, and everyone knew when something was out of the norm from the noise they made.

My grandfather's house was old, and by "old," I mean Colonial looking. It resembled a salt box house. Weathered gray in color, it appeared to never have had a coat of paint. It did not face the main road, but faced the south so you only saw one end of it from the road. The 1870 map lists the

McCready home as being there, so it seems that might be the same house on the old map, since the McCready farm is referenced in the Matthews deeds and will.

I was told there were twenty-five acres of land there at the time. Records reveal there were thirty acres originally, and it is unclear whether Daddy was deeded a couple of acres of land or just the house. I do not know why the second house was built unless it was to lure my father back to the farm with his new bride. I spoke with Aunt Josie about it, and that is the only answer that made sense to her since Pop-Pop lived in that large old home on the hill that he had inherited from his mother, Josephine Darby Matthews. I doubt that my mother lived in the house with Pop-Pop Grover, as she told me when she first went there, she offered to cook his breakfast. She said she cooked him eggs, and he did not like the way she made them, so he got up, went to the back door, and slung them out for the dogs. She said that was the last time she ever cooked him breakfast, but I do not remember them ever squabbling.

Mary Jo Matthews and brother Lake S Matthews

This was her plane and Daddy flew with her.

Welcome Inside our Home

The living room was furnished with stylish 1940s furniture which consisted of a burgundy sofa and chair and a navy-blue chair that matched in style. They were overstuffed with wood trim on the arms, and Mother kept crocheted doilies on the backs and arms of the furniture. There was a tall wooden RCA radio in one corner, and I remember being scolded for making noise when my parents were listening to the radio. They listened to *Amos and Andy* and some detective mystery, maybe *Elliott Ness*, that aired on Saturday nights, I think. Whatever it was, Daddy fussed if I opened my mouth when the detective story aired.

There was a tall metal smoking stand with an ashtray in it that we turned over more than once. Beside it was a short pottery lamp that had been a wedding present to Mom and Dad. Mother gave me the lamp years ago, and I passed it to Terrie around 2019 for her birthday. There was another lamp, a tall burgundy porcelain lamp with a Martha Washington image on it. On the wall was a long painting of a stagecoach on black velvet. Mother said that it too was a wedding gift. That painting made it in the move to Virginia, and I think we have a picture of it. I remember when the velvet got so thin that Mother finally did away with it.

Mother covered the old painted floors with ugly flowered linoleum rugs, upstairs and down. I hated them from an early age, but I am sure they were cheap, and I suppose better than bare wooden floors. In whatever areas received high foot traffic, the painted flower patterns would soon wear off revealing ugly dark-brown splotches of the linoleum underneath.

Once—later in Virginia—I was with Mom when she went shopping for new rugs for the bedrooms. The prices for full-size rugs started at around

$5.00 to $8.00, and I think the more expensive ones ran about $12.00. I remember they were on the floors in Granddaddy Alex Jones' house also, so apparently they were what Mother grew up with. I never knew there were cloth rugs until I went to my friends Brenda Adams' and Cookie Bradshaw's houses. They both had oriental rugs in their living rooms that were beautiful and soft on your feet, and you were expected to take off your shoes at the door. It's strange the things you notice when you are a kid.

In the kitchen, Mother had a kerosene stove with several glass cylinders for each burner and an oven on the side. The stove was white-and-green enamel. I would watch her fill the cylinders outside, bring them in, and flip them quickly so as not to spill the oil. One day, she brought in a big basket of crabs and was trying to get them in a large pot on that stove. I do not know what happened, but all of a sudden there were big blue crabs crawling all over the kitchen floor. She was hollering and putting me up on the kitchen table. I had never seen crabs before that day.

The white table and chairs were wooden with a porcelain top with a black trim that would extend with two leaves. Mother would paint the set every so often with a different color, and I remember her once painting it fire-engine red. When I got off the school bus one day, it was sitting outside in the yard, I guess for the paint to dry. I was embarrassed that we had a red table and chairs sitting in the yard. Another time, she painted it battleship-gray (probably the only color paint that she had on hand), and if I am not mistaken, it was yellow at one time.

There was also a slim white wooden cabinet with two glass doors at the top. The glass was trimmed in red-and-black swirling designs, and Mom would buy little decals of fruit patterns to put on the windows and on her other cabinet. At the time, women were putting the decals on everything in their kitchens, even the backs of wooden chairs. When Mom operated her furniture barn in Syringa, I remember seeing a package of those fruit-basket stickers. Mother kept all of the dishes in the cabinet with the glass doors, including a glass pitcher and little matching glasses with oranges on them. She kept items on the top shelves that she did not want us getting into.

The ice box was just that—a box filled with ice. It was white porcelain with a lid that lifted to display a metal-lined box where the ice was kept. The ice man would come once or twice a week and deliver a block of ice with big black wrought-iron tongs. Years later, Mom, Dad and I were at the flea market at Columbia Mall in Maryland, and I saw a set of those old ice tongs. They were $3.00 so Daddy bought them for me. That would have been in the 1970s. I gave them to Terrie for Christmas 2020 with a note about how I had acquired them.

The milkman delivered milk to the doorstep once or twice a week in bottles, not quart cartons, but at times Mother would buy raw milk from Roger Swift's farm. Once Wayne and I got a taste of the pasteurized milk, we did not want the milk that she bought at Roger Swift's farm. Mom tried to outsmart us by keeping a couple of those glass milk bottles. She would take them over to Roger Swift's farm and fill them with raw cow's milk, but Wayne and I refused to drink it. I remember her telling us it was the same as the milk that the milkman brought to the door, but it did not taste the same. I started looking for those little paper tops that you popped off so I would know where the milk came from. I'm not sure who finally won that battle.

Other deliveries were made at the doorstep, but I remember only one deliveryman's name. Mr. Byrd, the breadman, was my favorite. He drove a colorful panel truck that may have said Bond Bread or had a picture of a little girl on it. He would bring a tray of fresh-baked bread, and I probably remember him because he delivered our first box of donuts. He wore a brown uniform and heavy dark-rimmed glasses, and he had a treat that Wayne and I always begged Mom to get: chocolate-covered donuts. I do not think she bought them often because they were probably expensive. We loved those chocolate-covered donuts, and I still do.

The monster of all monsters lived in the original kitchen. That was Mom's Maytag wringer washing machine. She had to haul buckets of water to fill up that thing. She was washing clothes one day and went out to hang them on the line. I pulled up a stool or chair and decided I was going to run the wet clothes through the wringer. I got my hand caught in the rollers and it chewed up my thumb. I guess she heard me screaming, ran inside, and unplugged the monster. When she released my hand, there was blood and skin everywhere, and my thumb was lying wide open. Living in the country, she used what she had, pouring mercurochrome into the open wound. I remember that hurting worse than the wringer chewing up my thumb, and I screamed in pain. I carry the scar to this day, and when old age comes to visit, he attacks that thumb every time.

There was a closet under the stairway by the kitchen. Mother kept a curtain hanging in the doorway. Inside on a shelf was a white enamel wash basin trimmed in red, also a water bucket and dipper that matched the basin and a mirror on the wall. Since there was no indoor plumbing, that closet was where we took our baths, which explains the curtain over the doorway. Long shelves were loaded with Mom's canned goods, and I remember staring at all those jars of peaches. In the back of the closet was my potty chair, and I remember the spot well. Mom went to church one night and left me home with Dad. I was sitting on that potty chair, and within my reach, hung a string of drying hot red peppers. What kid could resist tearing those peppers apart and getting hot pepper oil and seeds all over them? I must have tasted a pepper because something made me cry. The more I cried the more I rubbed my eyes. Dad kept asking me what was wrong, but I could not tell him. The more I screamed, the more he spanked me, and the more he spanked me, the more I rubbed my eyes. Mom came home and saved me when she went into the closet and saw the torn peppers. I guess Dad was listening to his radio and let me stay on the potty longer than he should have.

One bedroom upstairs was furnished with Mom and Dad's maple bedroom suite that they had bought when they got married. It included a vanity and stool. I used to stand there and watch Mother curl her hair with a curling iron that would get so hot it would burn you if you touched it. She used to tell me not to touch it, and I found out the hard way that she was right.

She had a wooden jewelry box with a colonial scene on the top. She said it was a gift to her and Dad when they bought the bedroom suite. She kept that jewelry box all her life, and it was stolen with everything else in the house three months after she passed away. Of course, I always wanted to see what was in her jewelry box. One Christmas she got a necklace that could be worn as a necklace or a brooch and matching earrings. It was a large flower that looked like gold and had pink stones in the settings. One day I got a piece of that set and took it downstairs. I sat behind one of those big chairs and picked at that thing until I got out one of the stones. For some stupid reason, I put the pyramid end of the stone in my nose and could not get it out. In the panic to get the thing out of my nose, I pushed it up my nostril until it disappeared. I was afraid to tell my mother what I had done, and I was afraid I was going to die because I knew it was in my brain.

For years that thing haunted me. Every time I would get sick, I just knew that pink rhinestone, or whatever it was, would be the cause of my death. I was probably in my forties by the time I told mother about the stone and what I had done. I believe I have a high school picture with me wearing the necklace, so it must have been one of her earrings that I had plucked.

Mom painted two iron beds for our bedroom and covered all the beds with chenille bedspreads that would shed everywhere. I remember that the only other closet in the house was in our bedroom.

I do not remember sleeping in my crib, but I recall Mother bringing the crib mattress downstairs and laying it on the living room floor when I got sick with typhus fever. I was sick for a long time, and Dr. George Coulbourne came to the house to see me. I could only have warm lemonade and dry toast for weeks, and I remember begging Mom to let me have something else to eat. She would put my lemonade in one of her fancy teacups sometimes, maybe to help me tolerate the mundane diet. Dr. Coulbourne ordered big brown bottles of medicine from Baltimore City which arrived at Marion Station by train. I recall that once the medicine did not come, causing panic in the household. It was determined that a flea had bitten me that had come from a poisoned rodent and transferred the bacteria into my blood system, but I didn't learn this until I was older.

Apparently, people had nowhere to take their trash in those days, so they made trash piles in their backyards. Ours looked like a small mountain. Looking back, it was probably several pickup trucks worth of trash. Every once in a while, Dad would burn the trash, but the tin cans and other things that did not burn accumulated until something attracted wildlife. I remember Daddy, Pop-Pop Grover, and maybe John Barber climbing to the roof of the old shed and lying on the roof with shotguns. They did this at the edge of dark to watch for rats to move in the trash pile and shoot them. I did not like the sound of all the shooting and remember seeing rats running everywhere one evening as I watched from an upstairs window.

It must have been when I was so sick that I kept having the same dream over and over. The sky was dark blue, but there was a giant opening in the center of the sky that was bright yellow with sunshine and clouds in the sky, and Jesus stood in that opening. He was dressed in a long white robe and reaching out his hands. I had seen his picture in church and on the stained-glass window by the pulpit, and he looked the same in my dreams. There was a ladder like a swinging rope ladder that glittered. It hung from the opening where he stood and his hand was almost close enough for me to grab. From what I have read about near-death experiences over the years, I know now that I was knocking on death's door, or maybe I had arrived there but never made it up the ladder.

To this day, the virus information is kept in my medical records, and I have tested positive for parvo virus—a disease that kills dogs—numerous times. When I was twenty-one and and visiting my parents, I could not get out of bed one morning, as my entire left leg ended up paralyzed. Dad had to carry me downstairs. Before the day was over, the paralysis was taking over my entire side, coming up my arm and twisting the fingers on my left hand. They took me to Riverside hospital where the doctors insisted I had been bitten by a spider or snake from the tropics. I was hospitalized for a week or more and left with the doctors scratching their heads. I am convinced that the tick fevers I was diagnosed with six years ago started with that incident, and the many tick bites since caused it to surface.

There was nothing fancy about our house. There were three windows across the front upstairs and four windows on each end, obviously built with cross ventilation in mind. It was covered in white asbestos shingles, and Dad put sheets of tin around the bottom and painted them green to match the roof. He was always hollering when every time we played ball, we would hit a shingle and break it. He would wait a while and then replace all the broken ones at the same time, and we would start all over again. No one knew the dangers of asbestos dust at the time.

At one end of the house was a hand water pump that you had to prime. It was where Mom got the buckets of water. I do not remember the house being moved from the edge of the woods to the roadside, but I do remember when Daddy and Pop-Pop Grover walked that backyard with a switch in their hands waiting for it to point toward the ground so they would know where to drill for water. That is where the pump was installed. Using a divining rod was a very old method to detect water that I cannot explain. There was no indoor plumbing until the addition was built, and

Mother used to give Wayne and me baths in her big galvanized wash tubs. She would set them in the backyard and fill them with water on a hot day. After the sun warmed the water, she would bathe us there.

One hot afternoon a storm was rolling in, and Mom took me to the pump with her to fill a bucket with water. I was standing there watching her pump the water while it was thundering all around us. All of a sudden there was a long bolt of lightning near the pump, or at the pump, and Mom screamed but she could not let go of the pump. I still remember the fear I had as a child seeing my mother thrown to the ground that day. I do not remember what happened after that.

Although our yard had minimal landscaping, Mom and Dad planted two locust trees in the front yard and several running up the driveway with a cedar on the end that may have already been there.

The backyard had one old outbuilding and an outhouse in the rear corner—a one-hole Johnny house. Mom planted nasturtiums every year. Her mother had always grown them, so she planted them in memory of her mother. They were always yellow and orange, as I recall, and she also planted Mexican roses now and then. One time she came home with a cactus cutting that bloomed yellow flowers and big red buds on the leaves. That sucker had thorns on it bigger than a sewing needle, and she put it by the mailbox (J&W Seafood has a bed full of that same cactus out by their sign). It only took me one time to learn that reaching one of those pretty blooming flowers was like walking on a bed of nails. I remember crying when I got attacked by those needles and Mom fussing at me for getting into the cactus bed. She may have put the cactus plant there to divert Wayne from playing in the sand by the mailbox.

It was very hot in the summertime, but there was no such thing as an air conditioner back then. The fans were small and sat on tables, and we had a large one in the living room. Those fans are now hot collectibles, resembling pieces of art. Later on, Dad bought a large window fan that he would install in an upstairs window to pull the hot air out. He would open a small window at the opposite end of the house to create a cross-breeze. It would eventually cool off enough that you could sleep, but the best spot to be was sitting on the stair steps where you could feel the cool breeze coming up the steps.

Daddy hated a fly on the ceiling worse than anything else in the world, particularly when he came home to eat dinner. He would often repeat his claim regarding the flies, "first on the dog's ass and then on the butter," as he swatted with anything in sight. For some reason, the flies would cling to the ceiling. I do not recall Mother or Daddy cussing in our presence, if they did at all, but I think he did about flies in the house. His other rant when it came to flies was, "I had rather have a black snake in the house than a damn fly." Once when I was a little older, I thought he had lost his mind over a fly in the house. He got to the point that he could catch them bare handed and often flaunted his talent. I'm not sure what he did with them once he caught them.

Everyone had a big swab of white cotton hanging on their screen doors, including us. It was not pretty, but supposedly it kept the flies away from the door, so maybe they soaked the cotton in some sort of solution, maybe kerosene. Dad had one of those tin canisters with a pump on it— also hot collectibles now—and he would fill that thing with some sort of liquid and spray all the window screens at night to keep the mosquitoes away from the screens. I do not know what was used, but it sure did stink and would make you gag.

One summer afternoon, I was playing outside when the preacher stopped by. It was hot that day and Mom was in the kitchen ironing clothes in her underwear. Apparently she spotted him and thought he was going to knock on the back door. Instead, he took my hand and went to the front screen door. When I opened the door, he and I saw my mother running up the stairs in her pink underwear.

There was a large oil-burning stove in the living room that Daddy used to flood with oil, and the thing would roar until I thought it was going to blow up. He would open the drafts trying to cool it down. I hated when that happened and was scared he was going to burn the house down. One night his cousins Addie and Annie were visiting when Daddy messed with that stove until it seemed to be dancing off the floor. Whenever it stove was roaring and dancing, I would go stand by the front door, ready to run if necessary. When he opened the draft, a bat flew out of the stove pipe. Cousin Addie had silver curly hair and cousin Annie was dark headed. This bat was flying around the living room as the women yelled and tried to cover their heads, fearing the bat would get into their hair. Apparently, there was some old tale about what bats did in your hair, but I never knew what it was.

Mom and Mary Price (a neighbor) would go to the feed store for chicken feed that came in printed calico bags at the time. All the women who sewed made clothes out of the feed bags. Mom must have been into updating and trying to make our home pretty as she and Mary bought some feed once that came in a yellow-and-blue flowered calico bag. They kept going back to the feed store looking for more of that print so Mom would have enough to make kitchen curtains. She had an old treadle sewing machine, and, although she never learned to make clothes, she could do simple things like curtains. I loved to go with them to see the hatchery there with eggs under lights. I could stand there forever watching some biddy chicks peck their way out of the eggs and others that had already hatched and were so cute. There were numerous trips, as I recall, to match that yellow-and-blue print, but I do not think Mom ever found the same bag again.

Mom had a set of wooden curtain stretchers that she had brought with her from Baltimore City, and in the winter time she hung heavy drapes in the living room to keep out the cold weather. Come spring, she would drag out her lace curtains, wash and starch them, and put them on those stretchers out in the sun. It was a task that took her a long time since every piece of lace had to be pinned perfectly or the curtains would not hang right.

I do not believe anyone had potted plants in those days, but Mom would take a sweet potato and put it in a glass of water, and it would grow into a pretty houseplant. Someone came up with growing a piece of wandering Jew (so it is called) in water. It is a vine-like plant that blooms a little blue flower. It became a popular houseplant since it only required water, but I think the sweet potato plants were much prettier. I pull wandering Jew out of my flowerbeds every year and toss it, but I remember when it was prized. The only plant I remember seeing in homes then was a snake plant, but we did not have one.

Daddy used to do all the outside work. He had one of those old heavy steel push mowers and a handheld scythe for cutting weeds, or he would be working on his vehicles in the driveway. Mom was always inside. I remember her fussing with me because I always wanted to be in the yard with Daddy, not inside helping her clean. (Nothing has changed). If I wasn't outside, I was sneaking away with my books. The Hardy Boy Mysteries was my favorite series, not *Little Women.*

That said, I do recall one domestic chore that Daddy used to help Mother with, took pride in doing, and was a perfectionist at. There were no clothes dryers when I was a child, so all the clothes were hung on the clotheslines to dry. Daddy was methodical when it came to hanging out the laundry. He would start with the socks and hang them all in pairs, then on to the t-shirts, then the pants, and finally the linens. Hanging the washcloths together, towels, etc. There was no mixing of different items. When he gathered the dry clothes, he started at the opposite end of the line, working his way backward, and folding each piece as he went, ending with socks on top of the basket. He must have learned that from his grandmother, as Mother did not have time for such nonsense.

My mother had a fondness for flowers as long as she didn't have to grow them. A woman from church by the name of Hazel Wilkins grew rows of gladiolas. She would lay them in a flower basket and bring beautiful bouquets to Mom. Mom would put them in a tall vase and set them in the living room. Every fall, Cousin Annie would have beds of marigolds, the old fashion kind. The beds began at the porch by her kitchen and stretched all the way around the house. Mom would go there and cut bouquets. There was a lot of chatter about how pretty they were, but I did not like the smell of them. I still grow marigolds every fall and would take them to Mom when she was living. I have a plant of that old fashioned variety and try to gather seeds every year to replant. They still smell the same.

Mom would to go to a Black family's home down on the water in Marumsco to buy fresh fish. That woman grew dahlias and cockscomb, and every once in a while, Mom would bring back beautiful dahlias mixed with cockscomb along with the fish. I remember walking the rows of flowers with them as they admired the different colors and sizes. I do not know why the Black families always grew cockscomb, but they still do. Maybe it's a heritage thing passed down through the generations, as I have noticed it here in Middlesex also.

The woman disappeared one day, and it took a long time to find her. Mom was upset about her disappearance and would talk about it a lot. She would tell Daddy about it every night at the dinner table. I have no idea how much time lapsed, but the news came one day that they had found her body in the marshy waters of Marumsco Creek and said that the crabs had eaten all her flesh. I did not like the story and tried to figure out how a crab could eat a person. The story was terrifying to me. Mother went to her funeral as she did for all others in the community.

There were neighbors scattered up the lanes and across the fields here and there. Up a long lane across from our house were some of the Price families. That lane must have been two miles long, and Wayne and I walked it many a time. Halfway up the lane, Earl Price and his wife Peggy built a new home, and they had two young children, Denny and Cathy. Denny Price was a friend of Wayne's. You kept going and came to a Y in the road and if you took a left you would come to the home of Do Right (Arthur) Price) and Berky Price who had one son named Larry, also Wayne's friend. Do Right, a farmer, was Earl's older brother.

Once we had a big snow blizzard that made traveling an issue. Do Right had an old pickup truck and the night Berky went into labor, he could not get his truck out that long lane. He had to put Berky on his tractor and bring her to our house in the middle of the night. I woke to all the commotion, and looked out the window at the snow and the tractor lights. Everything must have worked out since Do Right and Dad left for the hospital, and Berky came home with a baby boy (Larry) sometime later.

One of my more visual memories from Do Right and Berky's house was hog-killing day. Yes, I got to see a huge hog that had been hung by the feet on a pulley. I don't know how long it had been hanging, but long enough for its throat to have been cut, and all the blood was dripping. They had built a fire and set big black cauldrons on it. They cut up meat all day long, as it was cold and dark when we came home that evening. Mother had the car loaded with pans of meat and entrails. I had been a fan of scrapple until I watched mother and Berky cut and grind all the extra parts of the pig, including its ears, and put it in the scrapple. Mom had taken every pan in the house and loaded them with scrapple to bring home. I remember she had it sitting everywhere in the kitchen, and I have no clue how she kept it, as they were no freezers at our house. That was the end of my scrapple eating for many a year after that.

The Matthews killed hogs also, but I do not remember witnessing the act there. Mary Jo moved to Nevada a few years ago, and, on one of her many trips to carry her personal belongings with her, she hauled an old black cauldron in the backseat of her car from the Matthews farm.

While they were busy working on the pig, the other kids and I were busy too. We found a litter of black kittens hidden somewhere and decided they needed a bath. I think I was the leader of that cruel act. They had a hand pump on the back porch, and I started pumping while Wayne and Larry helped me hold those poor little kittens under the cold water to give them a bath. Someone came onto the porch and caught us in the act, and we got in big trouble. I believe several of the kittens either drowned or froze to death from the cold water.

Back to the Y in the lane. If you took a right you could cut across the old tractor paths in the fields to Mr. Roger and Myrtle Swift's house. Mr. Roger, as he was called, farmed a lot of land. There was an old corn crib in the middle of one field with a big tree, and whenever we walked those lanes in the summertime, we would take a break at the corn crib to sit in the shade of that tree. When I was on the Eastern Shore in February 2005, Mary Jo and I went up the lane from the highway side past Mr. Roger's house. The little house was painted bright blue, and I did not see the other old outbuildings from the lane. I was able to drive along the tractor path, and there was still some kind of marker where the old corn crib once stood.

Directly across from Pop-Pop Grover's lane there was another lane with a big green house and the "colored" preacher and his family lived there. Reverend Alexander Reid and his wife Annie (whom I called Aunt Annie) had three children: two sons, George and Alexander, and a daughter named Charlotte. Reverend Reid was the preacher at Frog Eye Church, a Black Congregational church where the road curved in Marumsco.

If you kept going past our house, there was another old farmhouse up a lane on the right where Buddy Price, his wife Mary, and his mother Miss Ella lived. Buddy Price and his son farmed a lot of land and raised chickens. He probably had the most chicken houses on our road.

I can still see Miss Ella. She wore long dresses with high top shoes and cotton bonnets. Mary Price was the sister of Virginia Ward of Deltaville. Halfway up Buddy's lane, their son Copey had built some kind of one-story house where he lived with his wife Juanita, and they had one son named Bruce. I don't think they were any kin to the Prices up the lane from us.

On the other side of Frog Eye Church another one of Mother's friends lived. Her name was Marie Adams, married to Mitchell. They had three children, Gladys Mae, Ronnie, and Frankie. Frankie and Wayne were classmates. Mother and Marie were friends until the end, and Marie used to stop and take us kids to church, especially for Bible school if Mother had worked the night before. Mother got a Christmas card and letter from Marie Adams the year she passed away. I wrote back to her and let her know that Mother was no longer with us.

I have introduced the neighbors since you will read about them later, and maybe get a sense of their relationship to our family.

L to R - Mary Jo Matthews (b. 1944), Joyce Matthews B. 1943),
Ronald (b. 1946) and Frankie (b. 1948) Adams (brothers)
Taken on the steps of Lake and Margaret Matthews home in Marunsco, MD.
1950

MOVING ON UP

For starters, no one had televisions at the time but old Do Right Price went and bought the first TV in the neighborhood. There was a big boxing match coming up, and it was going to be on TV. I'm not sure, but I believe it may have been Joe Lewis (one of the famous ones). The Prices invited all the neighbors to their house for the event. Mom and the others took a dish of food, and all of us kids were going to get to play together. It was the first time I had ever seen a television set. Not only that, but Berky had a silver-looking martini shaker, and I had no clue what it was, but it was pretty. She also had a coffee table with a bright blue glass top that was unusual and had been moved to one side to make room for the TV. Everything was set up for a whole night of entertainment. The fight started, but as soon as it started, the bells rang and the fight was over. If I remember right, one boxer knocked the other guy out in the first round. So everybody ate and went home.

I don't know how long it took for Mom and Dad to get a TV, but they did, and I was there the day it was delivered. The first thing that came on that screen was *The Arthur Godfrey Show* and they were singing "Let's have another cup of Lipton tea." Mom liked *The Arthur Godfrey Show* a lot and we watched *Howdy Doody* in the afternoons. Later on, *The Mouseketeers* became an after-school favorite, and *The Ed Sullivan Show* was a Sunday night ritual at our house. It was on his show that I first saw Sonny & Cher and Elvis Presley. They did not show Elvis' legs that night because of his funky movements. Porky Pig, Elmer Fudd, Bugs Bunny, and Donald Duck were the cartoon characters of the day. In the evening, we were entertained by Gene Autry and his horse, Dale Evans and Roy Rogers,

Zorro, or *Gunsmoke*.

It was on that TV that I first saw the politicians that Daddy was raving about and presidential candidates, Dwight D. Eisenhower and some guy named Stevens. I remember the little round buttons for lapels that they kept advertising. Cigarette commercials were very popular and my favorite starred a guy dressed in a red bellboy uniform. He would call out something like, "Call for Phillip Morris."

Sometime in that era, Mom and Dad had a telephone put in the house. An old party line with numerous families on one line. It would ring two shorts for one family or a short and long for another family, etc. You could hear all these different rings, so you would know if the call was for you or not. I remember Mom fussing about somebody on the party line eavesdropping on her calls. I think it was Juanita Price. All the others were older and more respectful, I suppose. Pop-Pop Grover and Edna didn't have a telephone but would get calls at our house and someone would go to the corner of our property and holler until one of them came out the door, ran down the path, and crossed the plank board to take the phone call.

The TV was in the living room and the telephone had been set up in the kitchen, so that meant we still did not have inside plumbing. Baths were taken in basins and the kids in the washtubs during warm weather. There was a slop jar (as it was called) or a pee pot in the house that was brought downstairs every morning and emptied.

It was sometime after the phone installation that our parents built on to the house. They added a new L-shaped kitchen, a bathroom, and a small screened-in back porch. I do not remember the hammering and building, but I do remember the sink under the two new kitchen windows, and I remember the excitement of seeing the bathtub in there before it was ever hooked up. I would stand in the tub and dream about the showers I was going to take. Once the addition was completed, Mom was able to move the wringer washer to one side of the new porch. She had a rocking chair out there and my birdcage with my parakeet in it. She still had that wooden table and chairs as it was in the new kitchen when it was painted red. Sometime later, they bought one of those chrome kitchen sets with a yellow Formica top with six yellow-and-gray upholstered chairs with the nailheads on it for the new kitchen. The new addition was there when Hurricane Hazel hit in 1954, so that means it was built sometime before

I was eleven years old. My mind is telling me that the addition was added while we were living in Pocomoke City, so I would have been in the third grade.

I am assuming that Mother and Dad took out a bank loan to build the addition, as it was warm weather when some man came and nailed a pink sign on the front of the house that said "Auction." When I got off the school bus, I saw the pink sign and ran inside to tell Mother. She went out and took down the sign. In a few minutes the man returned and they hollered at each other. Then he nailed up another sign. Since I was young, I do not recall the results.

The addition also allowed my parents to move their bedroom downstairs. The living room went into the old kitchen and their bedroom moved to the old living room. I remember Mother had a daybed in that room in addition to the living room furniture. It had a light cocoa-colored cover with white stripes and round pillows for the back of it. Not only was Mother happy, but I was also because I got my own bedroom for the first time when I was about twelve years old. I remember them painting the walls powder blue, and Mom bought white sheer curtains for my windows. She left her vanity, mirror, and stool in the room for me. Now I was able to invite my friends over to spend the night, like they did me. Sueann Menzel and Brenda Adams were my best friends, and I loved going to their houses to spend the night. Of course, Daddy dictated who could spend the night. A friend, Helen Bell, visited one weekend and she brought makeup with her. We put on makeup that Saturday morning before coming downstairs, including eye shadow. Daddy was standing at the bottom of the steps and when he saw me with eye shadow, he tried to poke my eyes out with his thumb. He yelled that we had better get back upstairs and take that mess off. I must have been all of thirteen at the time.

Lake Matthews and his mother Amy G. Marshall Matthews
1940 - Crisfield, MD at home of Aunt Jose and Uncle Millard

OUR ADOPTED GRANDPARENTS

Remember the "Y" at the end of the long lane and the spot where we used to rest under the tree when we walked that lane? That was the home of Roger Swift and Ms. Myrtle. They were an older couple that resembled Jack Spratt and his wife. (He could eat no fat and she could eat no lean). Mr. Roger was a tall thin man with a weathered face, gray hair and pale-colored eyes. She was as round as she was tall with dark hair that she wore in a bun and little granny glasses. She also wore long dresses, black tie-up shoes and always had on an apron. They were wonderful to us kids and to Mom. They must have been her family-away-from-home, as we were there a lot of the time.

They had been married before, and they had three grandchildren who lived in Baltimore City. These grandchildren, Johnnie, Roger (Bunky) and a younger sister Jacquelyn Walker, used to come to the farm every year to spend the summer, and we played together every day. Ms. Myrtle had a son, Emory Walker, who wasn't there all the time. He may have been in the military since I have a faint memory of him in uniform. He drove a dark pickup, and there was a picture of me standing by him in front of his truck. I was young, and it appeared my hair was almost white from the sun. I do not know what happened to the picture. Mom used to keep her pictures in a dropleaf table drawer, and all the kids would get into them and tear them up. It irks me to this day!

The Swift's house was just a four-room bungalow with a screened porch on the front and back. There was a white picket fence enclosing a small part of the front yard, probably to keep the chickens and ducks out. The farm was everything that any child could wish for. It would have made Rebecca of Sunnybrook jealous. They owned every kind of farm animal that existed, and something was always chasing me and any other kid in its path. Not to mention the barn and the pastures and the creek (Marumsco Creek) that ran through the pastures, hayfields, and beanfields. All farmers used horses, as there were no tractors. The lane to the the Swift's house ended in a circle behind the house, and all the animal housing sat on the outside of this circle. The wagons, plows, and other equipment and a large woodpile were inside the circle. Also inside the circle, Emory made me a swing hanging on one of the large tree branches. There were black walnut trees there, and the nuts were laid out in the sun and dried to be used for cakes. I remember my mother cracking them with a hammer, and her hands would be covered in walnut stains that were hard to remove.

Ms. Myrtle always addressed Mr. Roger as "Dumbbell," and she would say, "you dummy." There was a big old wood cooking stove in the kitchen, and she kept a gray enamel basin on it with a bar of Oxydol soap for washing her dishes. I would pull up a chair to mess in that basin, and she would let me if the stove was not hot. At nighttime, Mr. Roger would sit in a chair in front of that stove and hand me a big black comb. I would comb his hair until he fell asleep. Sometimes it would still be daylight when Ms. Myrtle would fuss and say, "Go to bed, you dumbbell."

The Swifts grew their own potatoes, and Mr. Roger would hitch up the horse and wagon, and he and I would take the potatoes down to the woods where he would dig a shallow trench and cover them with pine needles to keep them over for the winter. Whenever Ms. Myrtle wanted a batch of potatoes to cook, Mr. Roger would hitch up the horse and wagon and we would go get them. I also went with him in the hayfields where he would pile the hay high on a wagon and take it to the barn to put it up in the loft with a pitch fork. I loved sitting on top of all that hay and riding on the wagon—a genuine hayride. He farmed a lot of land, and the crop dusters would come to spray all the crops. I loved to watch the planes when Daddy would take me to see the crop dusters early in the mornings. As we stood at the edge of the field, the planes dipped low and released a mist over the crops. I remember later in life reading about the detrimental effects of the DDT that was spread in the '40s and '50s.

The Swift's living room was next to the kitchen, and Ms. Myrtle kept flowered curtains hanging in the doorway connecting the two rooms.

Overstuffed furniture in the living room was also covered in big flowers. Flowered material was very popular back then. One day I went running through the curtains in the connecting doorway only to see Mom sitting on the sofa next to Emory Walker, and he had his arm around her. They sat in that living room a lot in the afternoons, but I hadn't thought much about it until that time because Mom—who did not smoke—was smoking a cigarette. The significance of the scene didn't hit me until much later because I was an active little kid with a big world to explore.

Mom and Ms. Myrtle would sit on the back porch and shell field peas by the bushelful to can them for the winter. I remember thinking they would never shell all those peas. I do not remember what all we had to eat there, other than corn on the cob, beans, and fried chicken, but Ms. Myrtle could make the best pitcher of Kool-Aid on Earth. She would slice oranges and lemons and put them in a tall glass pitcher with a lot of ice. It would make us kids drool when we saw it on her kitchen table.

In the summertime on Sunday afternoons, the Swifts would make ice cream, usually strawberry or peach, and it was so good! I remember their green wooden ice cream freezer and my dad being there to take a turn cranking the handle until the custard thickened enough to call it ice cream. When they would try to pull out the paddles, and met with resistance, the ice cream had thickened. They would test it and sometimes have to put more rock salt around the top and cover the salt with an old burlap bag. Then the kids would take turns sitting on the freezer as an adult kept cranking the handle. Later on, Mother would make ice cream at home and freeze it in metal ice cube trays.

Ms. Myrtle would grab a basket and take me with her to gather eggs. The henhouse, and the house where the ducks and geese lived, smelled really bad in the summertime. It didn't take long before I had enough courage to stick my hand under a chicken, feeling for eggs as she fussed and didn't want to give them up. I can still feel how warm the chickens were, sitting on their nests. Next, we would collect the duck eggs, which were larger than hen eggs. Ms. Myrtle would shoo the geese out of the pen so she could get the goose eggs. The ganders would stick out their necks, hiss, and squawk like crazy and probably would have attacked her in that pen. I was chased around that yard many times by a stray gander and still do not trust them. In fact, one got after me and the grandkids—Natalie and Ethan—this past summer at River Burch Petting Zoo. The last time we were there, an attendant told us they had put him in prison because he was getting a little vicious. Sure enough, we saw him in a goat pen squawking his head off.

The Swifts also had flocks of Muscovy drakes and a lot of Guinea hens. Muscovy drakes are not the best-looking ducks in the world. In fact, some of them are downright ugly, or shall we say "interesting" looking. They are quiet, certainly not threatening, and walk slowly. I don't think I have ever seen one run. Guinea hens are like watchdogs on a property. Nothing or no one comes on the property without the Guinea's letting the family know. Pop-Pop Grover had a lot of Guinea hens and so did Roger Swift.

Of course, to have laying hens, you must have at least one big badass rooster. Such was a huge red one that lived on the Swift farm. One day, I was playing outside alone—I do not know where everyone else was— when that darn red rooster started chasing me around and around the big circular driveway and would not stop. It must have been cool weather because the house was closed up. I screamed and screamed, but no one came to the rescue. I got tired of running but knew if I stopped, I would be pecked to pieces. As I got close to the barn again, I spotted a horse cart sitting there. I ran up the wagon shaft and jumped in. When I scooted to the back of the wagon, it went down like a see saw. I jumped off and the wagon flew back up. That's when the rooster ended up on the roof of the barn with a broken neck. I was so happy that I had out smarted him, but I doubt that Ms. Myrtle was happy...until that critter went into the dinner pot.

Speaking of dinner pots, there was always a small pot of prunes on the back of Ms. Myrtle's woodstove, where they were kept warm. In fact, I remember a pot of them on Aunt Annie's woodstove too, so just maybe they were on everyone's woodstove. Aunt Agnes and Mom-Mom cooked them also. I recall the adults eating them after their meals and not just for dessert. One time, at somebody's house, I took a bite. That was enough.

Another day, I was outside swinging, and out of nowhere, a big white Billy goat came charging at me and circling my swing. He got his horns caught in the chains holding the swing and could not get free, so round and round he went twisting that chain up to my neck. Emory came home just in time, ran across the yard, and rescued me from that crisis. I guess I would have been hanged by the chain had he not appeared when he did.

That goat was small compared to their neighbor Charlie Swift's big black ram with its huge rack of curved horns. There was a large pink rambling rosebush halfway down the Swift's lane, and I decided I was going to pick a bouquet of roses for Ms. Myrtle. Mom was in the house at the time. I went to the rosebush and was humming and picking out the prettiest roses. When I reached the back of the bush, there was that big black ram with his huge curved horns staring at me. All of a sudden, he was pawing his hoof into the dirt in full-steam-ahead mode. I suppose I knew he was going to attack by the way he was acting. I took off running up the lane with this bully on my heels. I threw my roses at him. Remember that white picket fence? Well it had a gate, but I did not take time to open the gate; I went over it. I can still feel the panic of that moment as Mother and Ms. Myrtle came to see what was killing me in the front yard.

There were two older girls who would come to visit from Baltimore. I can only remember the name of Dorothy. During one visit, we all got a bucket, pail, or other container and went down to a blackberry patch near the creek. The bushes covered a good deal of space, and there was an opening where you could get inside. We went inside and filled our buckets, but when we started to come out of the bushes, there stood a big black bull waiting for us. He, too, was pawing the ground with his hoof, but he was so big he stirred up a cloud of dust. The girls hollered for Mr. Roger, but he did not hear them, and that bull kept us trapped in the bushes for I do not know how long. The sun was setting, and finally somebody came looking for us. I don't think I ever went down to those blackberry bushes near the creek again.

It is a miracle that none of us ever got seriously hurt. The only bad thing that I remember happening was when the Baltimore girls and I were on horseback—me sitting behind one of them—a bumblebee stung one of the other horses. He reared up and threw his rider into the ditch. She might have broken an arm. I cannot remember for sure, but I recall her being tangled in the barb wire fence.

It was not all fun and games on the Swift's farm, for I had a daily job. Mr. Roger had a lot of cows—more cows than horses—and there was a fenced area off the barn where they would gather in the evenings to get their hay and water. Inside that fence was an old clawfoot bathtub and a handpump. It was my job to pump the tub full of water every afternoon for the livestock. Do you have any idea how many times you have to pull up a pump handle to fill a clawfoot bathtub? Well, I can tell you it is a hell of a lot. I would aim for the half-full mark and run to find Mr. Roger and ask if that was enough. He would come and look to see how much water was in the tub and say, "Nope, keep pumping." The old tub was orange from the iron in the water. Many times I thought the tub had a leak in it and that my skinny little arms were going to fall off if I had to pull that pump handle one more time.

Mr. Roger had every domestic animal you could imagine except pigs. I know because I interacted with all of them. Probably the only thing I missed out on was milking a cow. Mr. Roger was going to teach me how to milk a cow one day, and he got me something to sit on in the barn. He was showing me what to do, but I did not like touching the cow's utter and backed away. I never went back and tried again. I would love to be able to claim that I milked a cow when I was a child, but I cannot.

I have recently learned through research that Roger Swift was Pop-Pop Grover's first cousin, and I was shocked indeed. As it turns out, Pop-Pop Grover's father and George and Roger's mother, Amanda Hope Matthews, were siblings. The man who treated us like grandchildren was the cousin of our grandfather, Grover. Strangely, we never saw or felt one bit of affection from Grover. Now I am in touch with a cousin in California who descends from Grandpop George's sister. We are connected through a DNA test and shown as second or third cousins.

I also learned that Myrtle was listed as a servant in the home of Roger Swift, and that she and her three children lived in the home with him. It appears they married around 1940.

Probably as far back as my memory goes, Mom was a nurse. Mrs. Myrtle Swift kept me at nighttime when she worked. I do not know where Dad was. Mr. Roger would take the oil lamp into the bedroom, get into bed under a mountain of quilts, and when he got the bed warmed up, Mrs. Myrtle would tuck me in beside him. Mom would come in the middle of the night to get me and take me home. The only light in the room was a kerosene lamp, and he kept it lit when he got into that bed.

Mother drove an old black car that when you closed the driver's door, the passenger door would fly open and vice versa. She would make me sit or stand right under her for fear the door would fly open. There were no children's carseats or seatbelts at the time. I remember her saying to me many, many times on the way home, "See the moon, see the moon." I suppose I was just learning to talk and one night, when we were almost home, I looked out the window and said, "See the moon." I don't know why I remember this unless Mom was so excited and happy, she made a big fuss over my learning to put words together, that I never forgot it. I have no doubt this is the earliest of my childhood memories.

Rebecca had her Sunnybrook farm and we had Swift's farm. A child could not have asked for anything more, and the memories have lasted for an entire lifetime. I just wish all the children in my family could have spent as much time and experienced as many adventures as Wayne, Phyllis, and I did on that farm.

L to R - Phyllis Cline Matthews (b - November 16, 1951) Wayne Lake
Matthews (b - December 19, 1949)
Gloria Joyce Matthews (B September 10, 1943)

Children of Lake S. Matthews and Margaret Cline Jones Matthews
Marion Station, MD

HE LOOKS LIKE A FISH

I turned five years old in September and before Christmas Eve mother brought home something that I had never seen before. I don't know if I had been told we were getting a new baby, but Mrs. Mary Price stopped in front of our house with Mom sitting in the backseat holding this little thing. Dad was home with me, and we both went to greet Mom who was wearing a long aqua chenille bathrobe and holding a little red-faced baby dressed in a mint green sweater and hat that someone had crocheted. He had scales all over his face and hands and I was so glad to see Mom and was quick to tell her, "He looks like a fish."

He had a white bassinet like all babies, and there was a Christmas tree lit in the living room. A couple of days after they got home, Mom started down the stair steps in that long chenille bathrobe with Wayne in her arms. She had on silk stockings that caused her to slip and fall all the way downstairs with him in her arms. I remember the commotion as Daddy came running, but she never let go of Wayne.

Toddler Wayne was little, he was cute, and he was bad. I guess they moved me to the other bedroom when he was born because I remember well him being in that crib in my old room. I don't know how long he stayed in it, but he learned how to pull out the rails of the crib and throw them on the floor. Every time Mom put him in it for a nap, he would tear it apart, and you could hear the noise from downstairs. It wasn't long before they started calling him Tarzan, as he was always escaping.

Then came the pooping issues at our house. Mother was always a big advocate for healthy poops, and if you had a bellyache, you had best keep it to yourself. She must have had a bottle of castor oil in every cupboard, and if you even hinted that something was wrong, she grabbed it and the orange juice and the battle began. There is nothing in this world that tastes worse than that oily mess floating in orange juice. I soon learned to keep my mouth shut when my belly hurt, but Wayne didn't learn early enough. She got this big red rubber bag with a six-inch nozzle on it that hung on the back of the bathroom door. She would fill that thing up with soapy water and chase you down. I remember her chasing a screaming Wayne more than once. I know now it was an enema bag, and everyone you visited had one hanging somewhere.

It would not surprise me if Wayne developed some type of complex over normal bodily functions. Mother worked nights and Dad was there with us. As soon as she left to go to work, Wayne would poop in his pants. I remember Daddy would get so mad and search for the best way to get him cleaned up. He decided that every time Wayne pooped his pants, he would wash him in the yard with cold water no matter how cold it was outside. There was no water hose at the time, just the hand pump at the end of the house. I recall Daddy bragging to others how he potty trained Wayne.

I had agonizing earaches at times, but Wayne suffered from them often. Mother would heat up mineral oil, soak cotton balls in it, and stuff them in our ears. I don't remember fighting her on that one, as it was always comforting.

Somebody, maybe our parents or Mom-Mom Amy bought us tin toys that you played with in the sand. There was a Ferris wheel (now worth a small fortune), a sand sifter, and a couple of sand buckets and shovels. Mom would let us play with the toys by the back doorstep—there must have been sand there—but Wayne didn't want to play there. He wanted to drag the toys out to the end of the driveway by the mailbox where there was a lot of sand but also *real* cars and trucks. His friends were hardheaded also and would play near the road with him.

Mom would yell for him to come back to the steps, but he would not listen so she would send me to get him. There was just one problem. He didn't want me to bring him back in the yard. He always wore brown, hightop shoes. I would grab him from behind to pick him up under his arms, and he would scream and kick my shins with those damn shoes. This happened over and over until I was covered in bruises and scrapes on both of my shins. Mom solved the problem one day when he was fighting me. She went across the road, broke a branch from a wild cherry tree, tore all the leaves off except a few on the end, and swatted him on the back of his legs all the way to the house. Like I said, Wayne was hardheaded, so it became a routine event. I'm not sure how long it took him to learn not to go near the road. I had never seen a switch until then, but when he came along and started running around causing havoc, she mastered which tree branches to use for those switches.

You know that white slender cabinet in Mom's kitchen that had the red-and-white swirls on it and those things that she used to keep out of our reach? Well, I should clarify that she tried. Wayne would open one of the bottom doors and climb up in it, then open a glass door and try to reach whatever it was that we were told to stay away from. I cannot begin to recall how many times he turned that cabinet over on top of him, breaking all the dishes. Mom would run to rescue this screaming kid buried under the cabinet and all that broken glass. One thing I remember that got broken was that orange juice set. Mother had a pitcher and little juice glasses that matched it. She loved that set that was clear glass, with green stripes around it and a row of painted oranges. I do not know how many times my brother got his butt busted over it, but I do remember Dad getting in on the act.

Wayne must have gotten into trouble often as Daddy would tell him to "get upstairs." As he would start up the steps, Daddy would hit every step behind him with his leather belt, and Wayne would scream every time he hit the step. It always sounded like Dad was killing him. I remember Daddy bragging about how Wayne would cry, but Daddy never touched him with a belt. I wonder if he was ever beaten with that leather belt, the weapon of choice at that time, or just threatened. I am sure Wayne knows. No doubt, that act of kindness was passed down from Dad's childhood beatings with a leather strap.

All of the kids were over at Mr. Roger's one summer afternoon playing, when the Walker kids—the grandkids of the Swifts that lived in Baltimore City—were visiting. We were in a field across from the lane playing cowboys and Indians behind some huge haystacks. Someone had a BB gun, probably the one my age, Johnnie, and I must have been the Indian as they captured me, but I managed to escape. As I ran from the haystack, they shot me in the butt with the BB gun, so I made a beeline for the house. The more I ran, the more they shot me with that gun. Wayne and

Johnnie's brother, Bunky, were in on it, and I am sure they got their tails busted that day. Wayne still remembers this event.

Another day, we were climbing on one of those huge walnut trees with a thick horizonal branch. I could climb just as well as the boys, and when I got out on that big branch, Johnnie and Wayne decided they did not want me in the tree with them. Both of them pushed me out of the tree, which if I remember correctly, was a long drop to the ground.

Mother took us to Crisfield to see the circus one summer evening, and it had been raining for days. There were big old tractor trailers with the circus pictures painted on the sides of the trucks. When one of the trucks got stuck in the mud, they hooked up a couple of elephants to pull it out. As we stood in line to get our tickets, one of the elephants let out a yell when trying to move that truck. The bellow scared Wayne, and he took off running. Mother said she chased him up and down every street in Crisfield trying to catch him. I remember the trucks and seeing the elephants, but I cannot imagine her anxiety that evening. I heard her tell that story many times through the years.

As mischievous as my little brother was, I guess big sister stepped in once in a while to protect him. I saved both of our lives one day, and I doubt he knows anything about it. Buddy Price was renting and farming the land behind us from Pop-Pop Grover, and the fields were planted with corn. Dad was working at some garage, and he had brought a big wooden crate home that car motors were shipped in. He and Mom had put it under the last locust tree planted beside the driveway. The tree was the farthest from the road. They turned it on its side so we could crawl in and propped open the lid with a board to make a little porch. We had some toys in there and maybe a blanket for a little playhouse in the shade.

It was early in the day when we were in our playhouse, and that big truck of Buddy Price's, with rails on the side, turned in our driveway to go to the fields behind our house. I do not remember who was driving, but he ran over the end of the crate nearest to the house. I could hear Mom screaming for him to stop, and I pushed Wayne to the opposite end of the crate, cramming us both in the corner. I can still hear the crackling noise as the end of the crate was being crushed. Mom and someone came and opened the lid to the crushed crate to find us both still alive with not a scratch. I remember well Mom's panic and tears that morning. I have no doubt it was the end of us ever playing in those wooden crates.

Wayne had a little red tricycle, and I had a great big blue-and-white one. The only time we were allowed near the road was in the evenings when Daddy came home from work. He would take us on the hard surface road so we could ride our tricycles. I remember when I graduated to a red two-wheeler bike with training wheels, Wayne got my big three-wheeler and I was not happy. Of course, the day came that everyone thought the training wheels should come off, and so they did. I couldn't hold up that big bike and fell in the road, skinning my knees so many times. Dad would get out there and hold onto the bike running beside me or behind me, and I would take off. That is, as long as I thought he was beside me. As soon as I would turn around and see that he was way back there standing in the road, I would fall down again.

Once Wayne and I got into trouble at the same time. It was early in the morning and there must have been a pouring rain. Mom and Dad were at the opposite end of the house (where the pump was) working in the garden, and they probably had left us in bed. We came downstairs to find a giant water hole in the driveway. We sneaked out the door and got in the waterhole, trying to swim. I remember I had on a little yellow half-slip with attached panties and no shirt. There was an older man who lived beyond Frog Eye Church. Mr. Briddell was a big man with a bald head who still drove an old Model A or Model T car. He passed by our house and obviously caught a glimpse of us in that water hole. All of a sudden, he hit the brakes, backed up, and yelled to our parents that we were in the mud hole. Dad jumped all over us, and we both got our butts busted that morning. I never liked Mr. Briddell from that day forward, but I did steal his grandson's middle name and attach it to Steve. His grandson was cute, and his name was Milton Dale. We all called him Mickey but I borrowed his name "Dale."

Somehow Earl Price was involved with the Boy Scouts or Cub Scouts and he had enrolled his son Denny in the club. Wayne wanted to join, so Aunt Agnes had found him a shirt and scarf or a shirt and hat at the thrift shop. I don't know how often they met in Marion Station, but Earl would come and pick up Wayne. His dues were either a nickel or a quarter and there were times that Mom and Dad didn't have the money for him to pay the dues and were going to keep him home. Earl would lend the money for the dues and they would pay him back. Those must have been some tight times.

The first time I ever went to see a movie when I was a child was when Buddy and Mary Price's son Copey took Wayne and his son Bruce to see the original *Jungle Book* by Walt Disney. Copey Price invited me to go along to the theatre in Pocomoke City. I still remember the thrill of seeing the bear skipping along singing "Bare Necessities." It was wonderful and I never forgot it. I wonder if Wayne remembers it. A few years later, I got to see Annie Oakley in *Annie, Get Your Gun*, and then Juanita Price (Copey's wife) took me to see a movie that stared Elizabeth Taylor and a scary doll baby and *Cry Me a River* with Susan Haywood. They were intended for an older audience than me, but she must have wanted company.

Everything was geared toward the Old West when were kids, and Westerns were on our TV every night. Roy Rogers and Dale Evans were a singing cowboy and cowgirl that were married. Roy Roger's horse was named Trigger, but I do not remember the name of her horse. They had a short old man as a sidekick, and he was very funny. That was my favorite show, and I always sang "Happy Trails to You" with them at the end of the program.

Gene Autry, who was also a good-guy cowboy, rode a white horse. I cannot remember his horse's name, but I bet Wayne does. He also had a sidekick and I can see him now, but I do not know his name. I think Gene Autry was Wayne's favorite, and the boys would always get toy guns— cap pistols that were loud and threw off a little smoke, and holsters, and cowboy hats for Christmas. They were always running around with their hats on and sticks between their legs, and hopefully the fastest horse would get you where you needed to go. Then there was the Lone Ranger with his black mask and Matt Dillon of *Gunsmoke* shooting them all and never missing a target. I think that guy went on to become the famous "Marlboro Man" and advertised for a tobacco firm. I remembered him played by James Garner, but research revealed that the actor was James Arness. Then came Zorro, all dressed in black with a black mask, riding a white horse into the sunset.

Dad was just as anxious for those shows to come on every evening as we were. As a matter of fact, he got tickets for a rodeo in Delaware and took

Wayne and me to the rodeo. The main attraction was supposed to be Roy Rogers and Dale Evans but they didn't show up for some reason. We did get to see lots of cowboys riding bulls and horses that burst out of the gates. They would lasso baby calves and the cowboys and cowgirls did tricks with their lassos. I also remember barrel racing events. We were disappointed when Roy Rogers and Dale Evans weren't there, and I remember Dad trying to explain it to us. To this day, I wonder how often that happened and whether it was just an advertising gimmick to draw the crowd.

When Wayne started school, he could not pronounce his "t" very clearly, so every day his teacher held up a card with a tractor on it and asked Wayne what it was? He would answer "stractor," and I have no clue how long that went on. One day his teacher repeated the attempt to get him to pronounce his t by holding up the card again with a green tractor on it. Only by this time, I suppose Wayne had reached his limit, as he answered her with, "a damn tractor or a goddamned John Deere." I heard that story for years after that, and obviously somebody was cursing somewhere.

Wayne was a lot shorter than the Price boys, and when they came to play there was always a fight. Wayne would get beaten and come in crying. I remember Mother and Daddy telling him to either fight back or cry. I'm not sure how long it went on, but one day Wayne started swinging back, and both Mom and Dad said that broke up the fighting. It wasn't until after we moved to Virginia that Wayne got the nickname, Smiley. He is still known as Smiley today.

The Vietnam War was cranking up and the military draft was in full motion. Wayne was working at the pulp mill in West Point, Virginia when he went and signed up in the U.S. Army before being drafted in the military service.

Within hours of graduating from boot camp in Ft. Benning, Georgia, he stuck his hand in a fan blade in the dark, and sliced it wide open. His entire unit, except for one other guy and him, was sent to Nam, and Wayne was sent to South Korea. He served two years in the U.S. Army and stood duty on the DMZ line with the South Koreans guarding their border. Later, he became the chauffer for an Army officer.

SCHOOL DAYS 1958-59

Phyllis Matthews

Mom's Little Dust Mop

I do not remember the day that Phyllis was brought home from the hospital, but since I was eight years old and she was born in November, I was probably in school that day. My first memory of her was her scooting around the floor with nothing on but a diaper. She never crawled like a normal child but scooted everywhere on her rear, pulling herself with one leg. She would stick her leg out and then pull it toward her with her hands to create a forward motion and went everywhere. This vision of her was in the house at Pocomoke City. It must have been during warm weather since she was only wearing a diaper, and that was a huge old house. Phyllis had dark-brown curly hair and brown eyes. She looked like Mother and the Joneses. Later those dark curls hung down on her shoulders. Mom wanted to trim them, but Dad raised hell. Phyllis was the apple of his eye, and he made no bones about it.

Mom had an attack of appendicitis when she was about seven months pregnant with Phyllis. I remember Daddy saying that if they didn't do surgery she wasn't going to live, and if they did do surgery, she had only a fifty-fifty chance. I did not understand what fifty-fifty meant at that time, nor did I realize the danger that she was in. I don't know who he was talking to, but obviously they decided to do the surgery. When Phyllis was born, she had an "outie" navel and they always said it was because of Mom's surgery.

Anyway, she was born with this big ugly purple-grayish bubble-looking thing where her belly button was supposed to be, and the treatment of the day was to tape a silver dollar over it hoping it would invert. That meant she had to go to the doctor's office maybe once a week, and she did not want them messing with her. The doctor's office was in Pocomoke, and we would all pile in the car and off we went. I remember them taking Wayne and me into the examining room where we would sit off to the side. Phyllis was just a little thing, but it would take Mom, Dad, and the nurse to hold her still enough for the doctor to pull off the old tape, clean the area, and tape a silver dollar back over her belly button. She would scream, and it got to the point she would start screaming when we pulled into the doctor's parking lot. I am sure it hurt like hell when he pulled that tape off. I would get squeamish from the chaos in the doctor's office to the point that I hated to go. They used iodine for everything back then and that was probably the orange stuff that they put on her every week. I remember she always had on a little dress as that is how little girls were dressed at the time. I'm not sure how long that went on or how her belly button ended up looking.

Every week on a Saturday afternoon, Dad would take Mom to the A&P store in Princess Anne to buy groceries, and most of the time, he would sit in the car with us while she did the shopping. I remember the long waits in the car, especially since I loved to go in the store with Mother just to smell the fresh coffee being ground. It seems to me that she would take Phyllis in the store with her and leave Wayne and me sitting in the car with Dad.

It was hot outside, and Dad parked in front of the courthouse on Main Street. He must have gone looking for Mom and left Phyllis in the front carseat and Wayne and I sitting in the back. I was about nine years old at the time, which means Wayne would have been four. All the windows were rolled down and Phyllis was jumping up and down on the front seat when, all of a sudden, she fell out the driver's window and onto the cement pavement. Of course, she was screaming, and I was trying to help her, and all these people gathered around us. Phyllis had a purple goose egg that appeared on her forehead, and someone went looking for Mom and Dad. She had on a little green dress that day, and I remember the tears and dirt on her face and the goose egg on her head. When Mom and Dad got to the car, we were off again to the hospital or doctor's office. Thinking back, I am surprised that Daddy survived Mom's wrath that day. I just visited the courthouse in Princess Anne this past year, and I remembered the incident that had happened there more than sixty years ago. I looked for that A&P Store, but it was no longer there.

Mother would alternate between the A&P store in Princess Anne and the one in Pocomoke City. Daddy had a witty sense of humor at times. As he would sit in the car with us kids, all of a sudden you might hear, "She can't help but be ugly, but she could stay home." Of course, we were looking to see who was the ugly one. He had that label for a woman who lived near us also, but I will keep her identity secret. It is a miracle that we did not get into trouble at school for repeating his off-the-wall comments.

I have no idea how long Phyllis toted her bottle around, but she still had it when we were living on the Road to Frog Eye. I remember she would climb the stair steps with that bottle. Her bottles were the flat ones and you would pull a nipple over the top. The screw-on rings had not been invented. Once she reached the top of the stairs, she would throw it down the steps and break it. Of course, she thought it was funny. What may have started as an accident became a game with her. Mom would tell her, "Break one more bottle and that is it," and she would do it again. I guess Mom was trying to wean her from the bottle, but it did not work. Mom started putting her milk into those small green glass Coke bottles and putting a nipple on them. Soon everywhere we went, a Coke bottle went with us.

JUN · 58

Grover A Matthews and his pigs
Taken at farm in Marian, MD

Phyllis must have been born with an adventurous gene in her for when she was just a tyke, she decided to play with the baby pigs. To do so, you had to cross the electric fence, either over it or under it, and it sat close to the ground. Pop-Pop Grover had fenced a piece of the land not far from our yard, and he had pig huts there. A huge sow had baby piglets and Phyllis decided she was going to play with them, but the sow had a different idea. She attacked Phyllis in the pig pen and it was a blessing that Daddy and Pop-Pop Grover both were close by. I was at school and do not remember the incident, but I heard the stories of them shoving hoe handles down the sow's throat to get it to loosen its grip and how lucky they were that Phyllis had not been killed in the attack. Maybe Phyllis remembers the incident, maybe not.

Phyllis shared a couple of memories of her own and at some point, Pop-Pop Grover had drainage ditches put in around the farm because of all the standing water. We all loved to play in or around the big ditches at one time or the other, and Phyllis states that Wayne, Allen, and she were in one of the huge ditches sliding down the embankments into the mud when Edna came home after a trip to the dentist. Phyllis said she stopped the car and tried to yell at the kids for being there, but her mouth was full of cotton. All she could do was mumble and moan. Obviously, they thought it was funny.

Phyllis said that another time, they were having an egg fight behind a chicken house, when Pop-Pop came around the corner just in time to take the brunt of one of her pitches and got it in his face. I can only imagine his rage since he was a grouch every day over one thing or another.

One of Phyllis' acts as a teen has to be legendary at the home in Syringa. Phyllis took the little room upstairs as her bedroom, and she wanted it decorated pretty and painted a lavender color. Mother and Dad bought the paint, and it was Dad who painted the room for her. I bought her a white bedspread and white sheers for window curtains. It wasn't long before she taped Beetles posters all over the walls and on the ceiling, sending Daddy into a rage that she was destroying the newly painted room.

When they bought the house, there was an unfriendly black cat that hung around. I was sitting in the yard with my kids one day, and, for no reason at all, the damn cat walked up and attacked me. It must have calmed down eventually since it got to live in the house. On one particular day, I was there when Phyllis came home from school. She went up to her bedroom, and the cat was on her bed, but it had taken a crap on her white bedspread where the pillows were. She picked up the cat by its tail and twirled it in circles down the hallway. When she got to the top of the stairs, she flung it through the air and down the stairway, only it was flying above the steps. I have always heard that a cat lands on its feet, but I'm not sure if that one landed on its feet or its head. I don't remember where Daddy was at that moment, but when he heared what happened, we thought he was going to kill Phyllis for trying to kill that cat.

The older she got in high school, the more expensive my sister's wardrobe taste became. She wanted her clothes to come from Miller and Rhodes and Thalheimers Department stores in Richmond—like a few of her friends,

I suppose. Mother would contact me in Maryland and tell me what was on her wish list. There was a Sears Surplus store in Laurel, Maryland and I would go there looking for a certain pleated skirt, cardigan, turtleneck or whatever was on the list. I would buy it and bring it to Mother. One year she sent me to Leggett's in West Point searching for something at the last minute. Mother had a stash of the department store boxes, probably from Mrs. Lewis, a wealthy woman she worked for, and she would wrap the clothes in those boxes. They would have the store name printed on them in silver or gold. Phyllis never knew the difference and was as happy as she could be to look like all the other girls her age. Taking lessons from that, I did the same thing when Terrie and Timmy were in high school, since, God forbid, they were not going to pick out something from Sears Surplus to wear to school. I wrapped theirs in Woodward & Lothrop or Hecht's gift boxes.

Phyllis decided that she was going to attend college, but she only wanted to go Smithdale Massey Business College, the most expensive business school in the general area. Mother and Dad somehow found the money to put her there and she graduated. Her education has served her well.

Glenn Matthews Senior Photograph 1971

Our Baby Brother

Aunt Thalia Jones told me that Mother became really sick and the local doctors did not know what was wrong with her. She had been down for several weeks, so Daddy contacted her sisters Willie Mae and Aunt Thalia, and asked them to come to Maryland. When they got there, Daddy had made an appointment to take her to Johns Hopkins in Baltimore City, and they went with him. They did numerous tests, but had to wait for results and sent her home. Aunt Willie Mae asked her on the way home if maybe she was pregnant. Surprise!

So, when I was nine-and-a-half years old, we had another brother, and he would be the baby of the family. He was born April 26, 1953 and I am not sure why, but I remember the least about Glen when he was little than I do about Wayne and Phyllis. Maybe that old saying, "children are most impressionable between the ages of one and five," is true. I do remember that Glen had big blue eyes with long lashes and that he had lots of freckles. He did not have any kids in the neighborhood his age to play with, and I think he was always a good kid. I do not remember Daddy getting after him with that belt like he did Wayne.

Since the age difference between us was so wide, he was young when I left home and he was only seven when they moved to Virginia. I do recall that he was fascinated with the pigs and was determined to cross over that electric fence, and when he straddled the fence he would just scream and scream if his diaper was wet.

When Glen was born, Uncle Steve wanted to come see him, so Mom and Dad brought him to Crisfield to meet his new nephew. There is only six years difference in their ages, and they used to play together.

When Mom and Dad moved to Virginia, there were bobcats living in the area, and Glen was determined to shoot one. This was in the house that they bought on the hill, and Glen would go upstairs and look out the back windows with the binoculars until he saw something move. He kept the 4-10 loaded and sitting at the foot of the stair steps. He would come flying down those steps, grab the gun, and take off stooped down across the field. Mom said more than once that she was terrified he might trip and shoot himself. He never got his bobcat, but I knew they were back there because one had growled at Terrie, Timmy, and me when we were walking in the woods one day. We never did see him, but Daddy told us that he was probably lying in a tree and not to go back there again.

Glen got a job at the service station in Hartfield when he was in high school and worked full time in the summer. He dropped a heavy rim off a truck tire on his big toe, and his toe was swollen for days. I took him to see the doctor—probably Dr. Felton—in Deltaville, and when the doctor looked at his toe, he told Glen that he was going to have to burn a hole in his toenail to relieve the pressure under it. When Glen asked him if it was going to hurt, the doctor answered, "Hell yes, but not as bad as it does now." He came in the examination room with this round glass-ball-like canister that had a burning flame and a bent metal rod on the end probably six or eight inches long. The concept was to heat the rod and then stick the rod on his toenail until it burned a hole to release all that fluid buildup under the nail. I watched him hold the bar over the flame until it turned red and thought I was going to pass out at the thought of what was about to happen. I got up and left the room, but I could hear Glen yelling.

On another occasion, I had met Mom at Shirley Mears' grocery store in Deltaville. The old store was where that white building sits in front of Jack Hurd's house. Mom left with her groceries, and I went home with mine. She told me that when she opened the old pantry door to put her groceries away there was a big black snake crawling up the door inside the pantry. Glen was working at the gas station that day, and Mom jumped back in her car and went to the gas station to get him. The men at the station joked for years that Mother never even stopped the car but yelled for Glen to come kill the snake. He jumped the moving car, and she kept on going. Glen went home with her, and I don't know if he got the 4-10 or the double-barrel shotgun but supposedly, he blew the ass end out of the pantry killing the snake, and Daddy was pissed. Another night, Wayne came home late from work at the pulp mill and opened the pantry door to see a snake, and went to wake Daddy to tell him. Daddy would not get up, but the next morning he peeked into that pantry, and sure enough, there was a snake curled up on a coffee can just snoring away.

Glen graduated from Middlesex High School and got a job at the Newport News Shipbuilding & Dry Dock. He had been accepted in their mechanical drafts department and had bought himself a brand new Ford Pinto.

A normal adult life for Glen was not to be, nor was any normalcy for our parents for the rest of their lives. On a beautiful Sunday afternoon on June 23, 1973, he had dropped his girlfriend Kim Rogers off at her work in Urbanna and then went to watch the car races at Saluda Raceway here in Middlesex County. The race had ended, but a straggler race car rounded the fourth turn, and a back wheel came off and bounced over two fences and into the grandstand. Glen had just had his twntieth birthday. It must have been hot that day because Glen had lifted his shirt tail and was wiping his forehead with it according to those around him. He did not see the wheel coming and was not the only one hurt. A neighbor Tames Mears got a broken arm, and a pregnant female was injured.

We lived in Virginia Beach at the time and drove to Richmond to sit with Mother and Daddy that night while Glen was in surgery. The night was long, and Mother spoke of something she had never mentioned before: the deaths of her mother and sister. Out of the blue she said, "This brings back memories of sitting in that hospital when my mother and sister died in the automobile accident."

Glen's arm and shoulder were broken, and all of his organs had been pushed upward in his torso from the impact. His stomach was now sitting up in his chest. His diaphragm had been crushed and his spleen was ruptured and had to be removed. If that wasn't enough, somewhere during that tragic incident, he had a stroke and was paralyzed on his right side. He went through numerous surgeries during which his blood pressure would go so high, the surgery would have to end before completion. We were allowed limited time in the ICU with him, and finally, he started moving his hand a little and trying to stretch his fingers. We took that as a positive sign, only to learn it was a sign of brain damage. For months he lay there unconscious, hooked up to every machine available to keep him alive.

Glen was in the hospital for five months, and Wayne and I were there with him one night when a doctor came in. He said he wanted to show us something on a lower floor. We went with him to the basement to see a lot of young men lying in hospital beds breathing with the help of machines, tubes, and a small covering on their lower bodies. The doctor looked at us and said, "If your brother lives, this is how it is going to be." We left the hospital in shock and started back home. Wayne informed me that he could not be the one to tell Mom and Dad the news and that I would have to do it. I got him to agree that we would do it together. When we reached our parents' house, I got out of the car, and Wayne took off and didn't even go in the house. Mom and Dad were waiting for us, and I had to break the news by myself.

The next morning. I took Mother back to MCV hospital in Richmond, and once the doctors were told she was there, they wanted to meet with her. We waited in Glen's room until several doctors came and told Mother very gently that they could do nothing more for Glen and that they were going to send him to a nursing home. The doctors left the room, and Mother sat there in silence for a long time. I do not know how long she pondered, but she finally asked me to please get a nurse. The nurse summoned the doctors, and when they returned, she told them, "You are not putting him in a nursing home. I am taking him home with me." When we got home, she told Daddy what had occurred and he told her she was out of her mind, that it could not be done. Glen was still on a respirator with a feeding tube in his nose. He weighed only eighty-nine pounds on the day he was released.

Mother and Daddy moved their bedroom to another location in the house and had a hospital bed delivered to put in their old room for Glen. Mother would hear him crying during the night, so they moved in the room with Glen. There was a stream of physical therapists, and Wayne hired an RN to help Mother, as she was still doing private nursing duty at nighttime. Mother noticed that Glen started to sleep a lot during the day and was not alert. There was a gallon jug of red medication there for Glen which I think was morphine. Mother started marking that bottle, only to discover that the RN was giving him twice the prescribed amount so he would sleep. The nurse was fired on the spot, and Mother quit her job.

It was right before Christmas when we went home, and Glen's girlfriend Kim was there. We were all in the room with Glen. Mother had made her Martha Washington candy and it was being passed around. Kim sat on Glen's bed eating a piece of the candy, and broke off a smidgen for Glen and put it in his mouth. She went to eat another piece and Glen grabbed her hand wanting more, so she gave him another pinch, and Daddy started hollering, "No, he might get choked," but Mother was telling her to give it to him. Glen was determined and got another piece and Mother went into the kitchen, scrambled him eggs and put them in the blender. She then started to spoon-feed him and he was starving. She removed his feeding tube the next morning, cooked his breakfast, and put it in the blender. She even reached the point where she would blend scrapple with his eggs, as he loved scrapple. Mother said that Glen ate a bushel of sweet potatoes all by himself within a short period of time that winter, and she determined that the formula he had been given for six months was literally killing him. Had it not been for Kim sitting on that bed and eating that piece of candy, only God knows what would have happened.

It was thirteen years later when two men knocked on our parents' door on Christmas Eve. They were the paramedics who had taken Glen to the hospital in Tappahannock (the closest one to the race track) and then on to Richmond in June 1973. They informed our parents that they could no longer live with their consciences and needed to talk to them. They said that when they left Tappahannock hospital with Glen headed to Richmond, Glen's vitals began to drop and they could not keep him stabilized, so they returned to the emergency room with him. The doctor who had treated Glen there yelled at them, saying, "He is not going to live until you get to Richmond anyway, so get the hell out of my hospital." The paramedics stated that they went through living hell to keep him breathing, and he had quit breathing for at least six minutes along the way. It was in Richmond where the doctors at MCV revealed that the doctor in Tappahannock had run Glen's oxygen lifeline to his stomach instead of his brain, causing permanent brain damage for the rest of his life.

My parents called some lawyers as soon as the holidays were over and met with hurdles to try to right the wrong. First of all, the statute of limitations was long past, but worse yet, there was no record of Glen being treated at the hospital on that day. They had a record of Wayne being there, but not Glen. As it turned out, Glen had an old driver's license that belonged to Wayne in his wallet that was retrieved by emergency personnel that day. Glen had just turned twenty and apparently had found Wayne's old driver's license and carried it with him to purchase beer. Wayne did not know he had it. The doctor was located somewhere in Arizona and was no longer practicing medicine.

Lake Matthews and son Glen
Fisherville Rehabilittion Center

Daddy talked to each of us kids and wanted us to promise him that we would take care of Glen once he and Mother were no longer living and that we would not put him in a home if it could be avoided.

It was fourteen years after Glen's accident that Daddy left this earth, and until that night at the funeral home, Glen had shown very little emotion. We helped him stand by the casket, and he bawled his eyes out. It was heart wrenching to see.

Glen never walked or talked again after his accident, but he spoke to the world in so many ways.

Glen was good natured, and I do not recall ever seeing him get angry even before he was wheelchair bound, although he would get frustrated because he could not walk. He and I had many a laugh even with him in his wheelchair, but he and Phyllis were always close since they were so near in age. He would get tickled at times and let it all out in gales of laughter. One time in particular comes to mind. I had a good friend, Sharon Stork, who was like a sister to me, and she was no stranger at our parents' house. Sharon and I took Glen to Skyline Drive and into Luray Caverns one summer, and I was able to park down near the caverns in a handicapped parking spot. Glen's wheelchair was in the trunk, of course. I had opened his door and he was sitting with his feet on the sidewalk. When I opened the trunk to get his wheelchair, a damn bumblebee flew down my shirt and started stinging me. The bee had gotten into my bra and there was only one way to get it out. People were everywhere, since they also unloaded tour buses there. So, I crouched between my car and the one parked next to me and yanked my shirt and bra up around my neck. I was jumping around shaking everything, and trying to get the bee off me. By this time, I had been stung at least a dozen times. Sharon was bending over in stitches and so was Glen, and he never let it go for the rest of the trip. Despite all the commotion of my bee-sting entertainment, he did get to go in the caverns and see all the stalactites thanks to a handicap ramp in the cave for a short distance.

Sharon had been raised in a place called Hay Side, Virginia, and her mother still lived there on a steep mountain. One time we picked up Glen from a rehabilitation center in Fishersville and took him there for the weekend. Sharon took the wheel of my brand new '77 yellow-and-black Monte Carlo when we got to the mountains. The car had black leather seats, and Glen sat in the front seat. Who knew that Glen could get so sick from the motion of climbing back and forth up the side of a mountain? He threw up all over him, the leather seats, the black carpet, me, and everything in between, and there was nowhere to stop. When we finally found a pull-over, what a mess we had and no water to wash anything!

Still, Glen enjoyed the trip after that, and we were treated as family. Sharon's mother had a front porch and when it came time to leave, I feared Glen's wheelchair would keep on rolling down the mountain from those steep front steps. Thankfully, Sharon's two brothers got him down the steps and into the car, and once again, Sharon took the wheel.

Sharon had misjudged the time, and soon the sun was setting low and a heavy fog was rolling in. Out of nowhere, she told us to hang on, that she had to get us off that mountain before the fog set in. Talk about a joy ride! I moved over behind her instead of behind Glen and held on for dear life. What a relief when we saw the sign for Bluefield, Virginia where we got a room for the rest of the night. Glen laughed about his ride with Sharon for many years, and if you mentioned her name, he would do a hand motion like a snake and just cackle.

Glen Matthews

CHRISTMAS AT OUR HOUSE

If *Jungle Book* was fantastic our Christmases were tenfold better, and looking back, I realize Mom and Dad both worked at making them special for us kids. When Wayne and I were very young, Dad would take us with him down near the marshland in Marumsco to cut down a Christmas Tree. There was usually snow on the ground, and we followed him through that marshland looking for the perfect cedar tree. We stopped in at an old white farmhouse, and I don't remember who lived there, but Daddy talked with the lady of the house. She had a fish pond, and we saw these giant goldfish under the ice. I remember her telling Daddy how they lived in the pond all winter.

Our parents would take us to the firehouse at Marion Station, upstairs where the events were held. At Christmas, Santa would be there to greet all the local kids, and he would give each of us an orange or an apple along with a little box that looked like an animal cracker circus box filled with bon bons. I loved the vanilla cream ones, but somewhere along the way they put coconut ones dipped in chocolate in the boxes. I did not like them at all and would be disappointed, but Mom liked them.

Mom had wreaths that were covered in red velvet-like material and they all had a candle in them. I remember there was an orange-yellow bulb in each, and Mom would hang them in the windows and light them, and Daddy would put large colored bulbs on the cedar tree. I have no idea why, but he changed all the bulbs on the tree and in the wreaths to blue bulbs one year. I remember seeing bubbling candles in a store, and one year, Daddy bought a string. I recall our parent's excitement as Daddy added them to the already trimmed tree. They agreed that next year they would buy another string, and they did. They must have been expensive. I remember just lying there in the floor and admiring those candles as they bubbled.

It was a different scene at Mary Jo and Allen's house at Christmas, as the cedar tree would be cut, brought in the house, and set in the corner, but there were no lights or ornaments on the tree. I asked her why there were no lights and balls on the tree. It was tradition there that Santa would trim the tree on Christmas Eve after the kids had gone to bed. Mary Jo made a lot of colorful paper chains to be hung on their tree with the ornaments.

I do not remember many large Christmas dinners at our house, but for Christmas breakfast Mom would always make pancakes and sausage and melt a pie plate full of cheddar cheese, which was always a treat for Daddy. She did cook a goose one year and another time she roasted two ducks. I heard Mother talking about not liking one or the other because it was too oily. Maybe they were cooked for Thanksgiving, as I do not remember us ever having a turkey. I suppose if we did, it would have been a wild one.

Molasses was a big thing then and you ate it on your pancakes, or Mom would make biscuits, and Daddy sopped up the molasses with them. The molasses came in large red tin cans that had a Lion painted on the front. I think it was called "King Molasses." She baked her fruit cakes and made fudge and Martha Washington candy every year. Pulling vinegar taffy was a traditional event in the cold weather, and she invited a lot of people to pull taffy with her. Even her G/A class from the church, when she was the leader. They would stand in the cold giggling and pulling taffy. There is no doubt in my mind that she taught all the local ladies how to make it. She used vinegar in the recipe and once the candy reached a certain temperature, she poured it into pans for it to cool. When it was cool enough for them to handle, they would slather butter all over their hands, take it outside and start pulling. The candy would stretch until they ended up with long ropes. They would then cut it into bite-size pieces and keep it where it was cold. It was very, very good.

One year Mom had made all the goodies, and I went with her to get a round red tin box. George Reed (son of Aunt Annie and Reverend Reed) had joined the Army and was stationed in Korea. Mom packed the red tin with fudge and Martha Washington candy. I remember watching her cut a paper bag and wrap the tin before sending it to George in Korea for Christmas. Something registered with me at the moment, as young as

I was, and I believe it was the first time I realized how often she gave to others, no matter who they were.

She would wrap all of her gifts in white tissue paper with red curly ribbon and sometimes put some kind of Christmas stickers on them. Later she tied fake holly berries in all the bows. Popular gifts for women at that time must have been silk stockings and Evening of Paris perfume in those dark blue bottles, as I remember mother getting those gifts. I know at church the women had a secret Santa club, and mother was included. She would buy a gift for someone else and she would come home with a gift.

Buddy Price would take his big truck (the one that almost killed us) to the market in Philadelphia every week to sell things from his farm. and in the winter months, Mom would make Christmas wreaths for Buddy to to sell. Mom would turn the kitchen upside down every night. She would make her wreath forms out of some kind of switches that were flexible and then add bundles and bundles of greenery and bunches of red holly berries. Sometimes Berky Price would sit there to help her and sometimes it was Aunt Annie Reid. Then she would put everything together for the wreaths in time to get them on the truck. That is how she earned extra money to pay Santa Claus for the presents. I remember sometimes she was happy with what she was paid and sometimes she wasn't. There were times she would say, "It isn't worth what I am getting." Then, when they came out with the fake holly berries, it cut down on a lot of her work and time so she could make more wreaths.

The first present I ever remember getting was a gift from Mom-Mom Amy. We were at home and there were people there including Mom-Mom. When I opened my presents, there was a red calico dress with white sleeves and collar and a little peach-colored slip with matching undershirt and panties. The underwear had two little hearts linked together that had been embroidered on each piece. All the kids wore undershirts back then to keep them warm. I remember them laying my new clothes on the back of the sofa, and I just wanted to put them on. There was also a little gold heart locket on a chain to wear with my new dress that I think it was the gift from Aunt Agnes. I have no idea how old I was, but I do remember that Mom-Mom used to bring Wayne and me presents. After Phyllis was born, I recall hearing talk that there were so many grandchildren, she had to quit buying presents for us. I'll bet I racked up some loot in the five years it took

Wayne to get there. At that time, there were only Kirk (Aunt Josie's son) and me to buy for.

Somewhere in that time period I got a red stuffed elephant with a white trunk and big floppy ears, and I hauled it everywhere I went. I left it lying in the yard one afternoon and it got soaking wet and couldn't be saved. It was probably filled with straw as most toys were at the time. One of my favorite early toys was a pull toy that was a set of wooden ducks. There was a mommy duck and three babies walking behind her on a string and when you pulled them, they would quack. Phyllis and I were talking about it one day, and she bought me an identical set of ducks in Mississippi for Shannon to bring back to me. They had to be from the 1940s and I still have them. I also had a Sunbonnet Sue crib quilt that I hauled everywhere. It had a white background and got washed a lot. I guess it got ragged, but Mom kept washing it. Eventually my quilt disappeared, and I was upset about it. Even though I do not remember sleeping in a crib, I remember the quilt. I also had a big knot on my forehead for years, and Mother said it was from falling out of the crib and hitting her bed post.

Then there was my Gravel Gerda doll baby that I loved. She had long blonde hair, and she too got left in the backyard and rained on. I don't know what was inside her rubber body, but the rain made her heavy and stiff.

Christmas in the first grade was one for the memory books. Mom and Dad had friends, Reds and Beatrice Renshaw, who lived over near Shelltown, and that summer lightning hit their house and burned it to the ground. They had one son named Butch, or that is what they called him anyway. After the house burned, they came to live with us. Butch and I started first grade together, and they were still there at Christmas. I got my only dollhouse that year, also a bride doll, and my first baton. The reason I remember so well is that Butch got a barn with all the animals, tractors, etc. Between the dollhouse and the barn, we set up a big farm and he and I took up the entire living room floor with all the stuff that Santa had brought.

Santa was fat one year, and I got a wooden table and chairs and a set of green jadeite glass dishes. That same year I got a baby doll with long blonde pigtails. I remember well her having a blue printed dress and bows tied on her pigtails, a straw hat, and a blue metal stroller (just like Mom had). She was a stiff doll, but her arms and legs would bend. Wayne and I would play house, and we had to be careful with the dishes as they would break. I would be the mommy and he was the daddy.

I don't know how old we were, but Wayne had two friends who lived down the road, Ronnie and Frankie Adams. Ronnie had dark hair and eyes and Frankie had red hair and freckles and obviously a temper to go with the red hair. Mom had set my table and chairs in the kitchen one summer day by the screened back door. Wayne and I were playing house when Marie Adams stopped in with the two boys. Something rocked Frankie's boat, and he picked up my table and turned it over, breaking all my dishes. I was not a fan of Frankie Adams from then on.

When I got a little older, paper dolls were the rage, and I had a lot of them. There were paper dolls that looked like we did as young kids on up to paper dolls that were dressed in ball gowns. They were fun to play with and occupied little girls for hours.

Since TV entertainment in the evenings was always Westerns, at least at our house, Wayne and his friends were usually playing like cowboys and Indians. Consequently, their wishlist consisted of pistols in holsters. They had pistols that shot paper caps, and wore cowboy hats, vests and chaps. After Santa came, the western front was very active and loud. Wayne, the Price boys, Larry and Denny, the Adams brothers, and, more than likely Allen Matthews ran around the yard hiding and ambushing each other with those paper cap pistols. I guess there were good guys and bad guys. I remember they would run around with a long stick or branch between their legs and go as fast as their horses could run. Oh yeah. They got handcuffs also and would lock each other up. Later on, they all wanted the rifles that shot BBs, and Wayne got his. He got a red tricycle one year, and either he or Glen got a red flyer wagon from Santa. That might have been Glen, as it came from Western Auto in Virginia, I believe. Wayne learned to ice skate somewhere, and one year he got ice skates for Christmas.

One Christmas the only thing I wanted and asked Santa for was a scooter. They were gray metal with red wheels and a red handlebar. When I woke up that morning, Santa had been there but did not bring me the scooter. I didn't understand why. Dad got up and went somewhere and came back with the scooter that I wanted. He said that Santa had left it over to Mr. Roger and Myrtle's house. I guess they forgot it!

Beatrice Renshaw and Phyllis Cline Matthews
Taken at home of Lake and Margaret Matthews
Marion, MD
Everybody drove a Ford - the dark colored one was Lake's car.

The Christmas when I was in the fourth grade also stands clearly in my mind. I am not sure why I remember some and not others, but at this time we were living in Pocomoke City (209 Linden Avenue). Dad had gotten a job there and had rented a big old Victorian house that we loved. I have figured out that I was in the third grade when we moved, so that would have been 1951. There was a lane that ran by the house, and a couple by the name of Earl and Betty Stanton lived there. Apparently, Betty was a crafter. That Christmas I got a Tiny Tears doll baby (my last doll baby) that cried real tears. For a doll bed, Betty took a little oval vegetable basket, made a mattress for it, and covered the basket in a pink fabric trimmed in blue ric-rac. It had a ruffled cover all the way around it. Then she made a nightgown, blanket, and pillow. I thought it was wonderful.

For Phyllis, Betty took a cardboard box and covered it in pink paint, cut a hole in the top, and glued big ABCs all over the box. I remember watching her and Mom filling the box with rattles, blocks, and other toys for Phyllis. I do not remember what she did for Wayne, but I'm sure it was something. Glen had not been born at that time. Of course, the only thing I ever remember Wayne wanting were things that said Gene Autry. I do remember him getting a light green Ford car that year that you would push two or three times on the floor and it would take off all the way across the room. That may have also been the year that he got the service station with all the cars, trucks, and wreckers. I know Dad brought home a rubber tire with an ash tray in the center, and he and Mom had gone to a Christmas party where he worked.

When I got a little older Mom would get me a Charm Doll from a different country every Christmas, each one in her native dress. I must have collected ten or twelve of them. Everywhere I moved I took a box with my Tiny Tears doll and all my Charm Dolls with me. When Jerry and I lived in a house in Crisfield the box was in the attic and somehow got left behind. My three kids were all under age five, and my mind was somewhere else. I tried to locate my dolls but was not successful.

I must have been in the sixth or seventh grade when I got my Charm Doll and a gold-colored fake leather jacket and a brown straight skirt with a kick pleat in the front, but then I got a long-sleeve pink, Ivy League blouse and I was bothered that my blouse did not match my jacket, but I didn't say anything. We went to North Carolina that year for Christmas and Mom let me wear my new outfit. I thought I was hot stuff strutting around on that ferry boat.

The last Christmas I was home, I got a Brownie camera and it wasn't even wrapped but just handed to me in the box. That was no fun. I resented it because the younger kids' gifts were wrapped, but not mine.

There was always a program and play at our church, Rehobeth Baptist during the holidays as well as at the school. I remember as kids we would be included in the plays, dressing as shepherds, wisemen, or angels as we re-enacted Jesus being born and laid in the manger. The choirs would sing Christmas carols and at one school concert, I heard a friend, Brenda Adams, sing, "Oh Holy Night," and it became one of my favorite Christmas carols. It still is.

One Christmas Eve, Daddy came from Pop-Pop Grover's house and brought a child's black Boston rocker that was trimmed in gold paint, a red fire engine that you rode on, and a little stuffed horse on wheels that was a pull toy. I remember that Wayne was tall enough to ride on the firetruck. I learned later that all three of the toys were from Daddy's childhood, presents that Santa had brought him. It was an indication that he had gotten some nice gifts when he was a child.

One of my favorite Christmas memories is one spent with Dad on Christmas Eve. I worked at G.E.X. in Hampton, Virginia, and I would usually take the Greyhound bus to Saluda on Friday night where Dad would meet me. I had to work until 6:00 pm on Christmas Eve so he drove to Hampton to pick me up. It was snowing when he got there, so we quickly went to where I lived and loaded up the car. I had bought the kids a table and chairs that year, along with dolls, G.I. Joes, trucks or whatever was the rage, and gifts for family. The trunk and the backseat were full and we headed back to Syringa in a blizzard. As we crossed the Coleman Bridge over the York River it was really bad, and we kept hitting whiteouts making it a long trip home. We made it all the way to the bottom of Mom and Dad's lane and we could not get up the icy hill, so Dad had to park the car at the end of the lane. We took what we could, and started walking up the lane, and it would take us two or three more trips to take everything to the house. The moon was bright that night and lit up the snow, smoke was coming out of the chimney, and by this time there was just a light snowfall. It was quiet and serene, and the entire scene was right out of a Norman Rockwell painting. If you have ever listened to the words, "Silent Night," Dad and I were living it at that moment. It's a memory that I have always held close to my heart.

Some Years the Easter Bunny Forgot to Hop

We were always in church on Easter Sunday dressed in our Sunday best and then went to Mom-Mom Amy and Aunt Agnes' house in Crisfield that afternoon. One Easter, I had a two-piece gray suit with a little red plaid trim around the jacket collar and pockets, but I didn't have a bonnet to wear to church. Aunt Agnes went to the thrift store and bought me a straw hat with a rolled brim, and Mother went to W. T. Grants on Main Street and got a little bouquet of red flowers and some red ribbon. That Saturday afternoon, they sat at Aunt Agnes' and worked on my straw hat. The next morning, Wayne and I sat on the front church pew. He was dressed in a suit, hat, and tie, and I was in my suit and straw hat. We were proud of how dressed up we were, and it all probably came from the thrift shop, or hand-me-downs from somebody.

One Easter Sunday I had a fancy flowered dress with a big bow on the back that Mom-Mom had probably bought for me, and we were out playing in Mom-Mom Amy's front yard that afternoon with the kids in the neighborhood. The adults were sitting on the front porch, and I leaned up against a light pole that had just been covered in tar. I remember the commotion as they stripped off my dress and tried to find something to take the black tar out of it. I don't know if they were able to save it or not.

One of the few times I remember Glen as a small child, the entire family had gone to Ocean City on Easter Sunday. They used to have Easter parades there on the boardwalk, and everyone would deck out trying to win a prize for the best Easter bonnet. There was an old song that was popular that went, "In your Easter bonnet, with all the frills upon it, you'll be the grandest lady in the Easter parade." I guess that was the goal on the boardwalk.

There was a woman, named Hattie Swift, who lived not too far away who was a seamstress. Mother bought a pink piece and a yellow piece of pique fabric and had her make Phyllis and me matching dresses. Phyllis got the pink one and I got the yellow one and they were pretty with full skirts and big bows in the back. On the collars, Hattie had embroidered little flowers. I remember us walking that boardwalk where everybody was dressed up, and Glen was in one of those old blue-and-white metal strollers. We sat on the benches along the boardwalk and watched all these women walking by in big hats and fox tails draped around their necks. That must have been quite an outing for Mom...or maybe not with four kids! It had to have been a family event, as I remember others being there, including Aunt Agnes and Aunt Josie, I believe.

Mother would fuss if Easter fell in March or the first of April rather than the end of the month. She would say it was too cold. Everyone would have to wear a coat. Years later, she would get a *Spiegel Catalog* in the mail and, depending on when the holiday fell, she would order herself, Phyllis, and me a topper from the catalog. A topper was a coat that hit just at the hips and usually had big pockets. I remember one year, Mom ordered all of us an aqua topper for Easter, and the women always wore corsages to church on Easter Sunday. You wore one color (probably the white ones) if your mother was deceased and yellow or red if they were living. On second thought, maybe that was for Mother's Day, which would make more sense.

The Easter Bunny brought us Easter baskets if he didn't forget, and one year, he did just that. It was a sad morning when Wayne and I went looking and found nothing. Once again, Dad got in the car and went somewhere, but this time, he came back with one metal sand bucket with a few jelly beans in it, and even they were sparce, believe me. There wasn't even any straw in the bucket, just a few jelly beans rolling around in the bottom of it. I have never even liked jelly beans.

We were sitting upstairs on our bed with that bucket, looking at those few jelly beans, and I wonder what we were thinking. I kind of have the feeling that when Mom was working nights, Dad was supposed to take care of this stuff and sometimes didn't come through.

One year, Daddy came home and told us that he had seen the Easter Bunny lying dead in the road, and that somebody had run over him with their car. I guess he thought that was cute, but we were upset that the

Easter Bunny had died. Another year, Wayne and I found big baskets hidden behind a living room chair. They were tied in yellow cellophane with large bows and we both sat behind that chair and had a feast until Mom caught us.

Miss Myrtle Swift would make homemade Easter eggs and dip them in chocolate. Miss Myrtle had a mold of a chicken, and she made me a chicken covered in chocolate and put eyes and a mouth on it. That night I was exhausted and set my Easter basket on the floor next to the sofa while I took a nap. When I woke up, my puppy, Laddie, had eaten my entire chicken, and yes, the tears just rolled and I wonder where Mom and Dad were that they didn't see the dog eating my chicken.

I do not ever remember a Halloween that we dressed up in costume and went trick-or-treating. The first Halloween event that I ever remember was at Rehobeth Baptist Church when I was a teen. I guess we lived too far out in the boonies to celebrate that holiday. As a matter of fact, I do not remember seeing a pumpkin or Jack-o-Lantern, and I now wonder if they were a no-no in the Baptist Church. I do remember Mother having an apple-bobbing contest for the girls in the G.A. group at our house, where she would fill up a wash tub with water and dump a basket of apples in the tub. The girls had to grab them with their mouths, holding their hands behind their backs, and it looked like so much fun. I watched from a distance and maybe I knew those older girls would have pushed my head in that tub of water. Maybe that was for Halloween.

Joyce Matthews
First Grade

THE COLORED FOLKS

There were Black families that lived throughout the area in the old houses just like the White folks. No one had a designated area. They were referred to as colored people. Along with them, a neighbor, Buddy Price, would bring in migrant workers in the summer months to harvest his crops. He would load hay bales in the back of that big truck with the sides for them to sit on during the journey, and there was a tarp that covered the entire back of the truck in case of rain. I believe I remember talk of him going to either North or South Carolina to get the workers, and many must have returned year after year. I would be out in the front yard playing when the truck would pass our house, and they would be standing up on the hay bales and would holler and wave to me.

Buddy Price had lots of chicken houses and he planted strawberries, tomatoes, and peppers. Mother would go there at harvest time and help his wife, Mary, in the shanty where they weighed and counted the produce. The fields were full of the migrants bent over on every row, and the colored kids and I would play and eat strawberries. I remember how hot the sun was and how dirty we would get. There was one little girl I played with a lot. We went to her house on the farm to play. It was a two-story house and the door was always wide open. She came up with this piece of material and the biggest pair of scissors I had ever seen and told me that she was going to make me a new dress, but she had to cut my dress off to make a pattern. She started coming toward me with those scissors and scared me to death, so I ran out the door, and I don't think I ever went back into that house again. I wasn't afraid that she was going to hurt me. I just didn't want her cutting my dress.

The Prices had a colored man, named Lem, who called the farm home. Mary Price had a huge pantry off her kitchen and there was a small table and a stool in there for Lem to sit on. Every night, Lem would go in the pantry to eat his supper that Miss Mary or his mother, Ella Price, had cooked that day. It did not matter how good the relationship was, the white folks and the colored folks did not eat at the same table.

Mother had been there on this particular day helping the ladies wallpaper the old kitchen, and we were there eating supper. Lem was in the pantry cleaning pig's feet and he would come out and show the pig's foot to Buddy at the table and ask if the foot was clean enough. Lem would then go back into the pantry and scrape those feet with a razor some more. Finally, he would emerge with a pig's foot that looked like it had been bleached, and not a hair to be found. This would have been in the dead of winter, as that is when they killed hogs.

How do I know they wallpapered the kitchen that day, you ask? Miss Ella did not want to eat supper until the wallpapering job was completed, so we ate supper there that evening so Mom could help her finish the papering. There was no scaffolding to stand on to reach the tall walls, so they brought in fifty-five-gallon drums and laid wide boards across them for the women to stand on, one on each end. I can clearly see Miss Ella standing on that board as she brushed out all the wrinkles in the corner by the pantry while we were eating at the kitchen table. Lem was there in the pantry eating, and they tried to talk her into taking a break to eat. The vision of her may be clear to me because of the way she dressed. She still wore long dresses and black tie-up shoes with a short heel but the thing that stuck out the most were her bonnets. You never saw Miss Ella without her bonnet with the long flap that covered her neck. If you have paid attention to the old Western movies and the way the ladies were dressed, that was Miss Ella. One would have been convinced that she just climbed off the covered wagon.

There was another family that lived close by, and they might have worked for Buddy Price also, but I am not certain. Her name was Mitsy Burgess, and she would walk by our house going to the store. She was a petite woman and always stopped in the road to talk to Mother and me.

When we lived in Howard County, MD, I decided to take my kids down to Somerset County to show them where I was born and raised. I was anxious, as I had not been to the shore for years, and, even though the kids visited Crisfield often, they had never been to Marumsco. We turned onto the Road to Frog Eye Church and it was only a short distance to the old house.... Bam! It was gone. There in its tracks was a small new bungalow with a huge tractor trailer in the driveway. We pulled in, I got out of the car, and, as I stood there knocking on a stranger's door, I had no clue what I was doing or what I was going to say. The door opened and a petite older Black lady answered the door, so I started blabbing that I had been born in the old house that used to be there and had brought my kids to show them where I was raised. I asked if she had known the family that lived there. She looked up at me and said, "Joyce." I did not recognize her, but it was Mitsy Burgess. She told me that the old house had been torn down some years ago and that her son had built her the new one. Her son was the long-haul driver who owned the rig sitting in the driveway and that he was sleeping. "Get your husband and kids out of that hot car," she insisted. "Get up here in the shade."

We talked and talked—about what, I cannot tell you, except that I told her I wished I had known the house had been demolished and that I would like to have had a brick from the old chimney. She stood, went and got a shovel, and motioned for me to follow her. Around the side of the house was a flowerbed neatly lined with bricks. They had been set halfway in a trench and were leaning on an angle, so Mitsy started digging. Something like four or five bricks went into the trunk of my car that day and made it back to the garage on Feathered Head. Somewhere down the road, my ex brought more bricks home and added them to my little stack. I lined a flowerbed with those bricks, but eventually they got in the mix, and I lost tracks of the old ones.

One time, Mary Jo was visiting us here in Virginia, and I happened to remember Mitsy Burgess. I told Mary Jo the story regarding the old bricks, and said that Mitsy had probably been dead for years. Much to my surprise, Mitsy was still living in the little house, and Mary Jo commented she has to be close to 100 years old by now.

When you went out of our road on the highway and took a left, there was the only store close to us, and it was owned by a man named Lawrence Burgess. In fact, I believe it took on the name Burgess Corner and might be called that to this day.

Behind that store and behind his house that sat across the road, there were rows of chicken houses that Pop-Pop Grover rented. Daddy used to go there to feed and water the chickens.

I do not know why, but some of the feed rooms at the end of the chicken houses had been turned into living quarters for some of the "colored" folks. There was a woman who lived in the feed room at that location by the name of Charlotte Taylor. I remember being in that room after dark with Charlotte cooking supper, while Daddy was feeding the chickens. So, she was set up to be independent. Mother would hire Charlotte to come and help her do things at our house on occasion, and Daddy used to take her in the car if she needed to go somewhere.

Mother always bought nuts at Christmas to bake with and others just for eating. My favorite in the batch were Brazil nuts, and somewhere along the way they were tagged as "Negro toes." That may have been what our parents called them, but I am not sure. What I am sure of is that Charlotte was coming to the house to help Mother do something, and she warned me not to get Charlotte to crack me any nuts. She was in that closet under the stairs doing something, when I grabbed a handful of those nuts and went running to asked her if she would crack me a Negro toe. No doubt I did not pronounce the word correctly and got into trouble with Mom.

There was another incident that I recall with the migrant workers. There was an old home that may have been a plantation at one time, and you could just see the roof from our back door over the trees. A couple lived there, and they, too, used to walk up and down the road all the time going to Burgess Store. I never knew the full story, but they got into a fight and the man shot the woman in the stomach and then fled. The only thing that she could reach was an egg, so she put an egg in the hole in her stomach to keep from bleeding to death. I guess Buddy Price went looking for them a few days later and found her that way. He told the story of how he removed the egg and stuffed rags into the hole until they could get the woman to the hospital. I have no clue about the outcome of that story.

Then there were the stories of the "colored" ladies whom I loved, and they loved me. I spoke of Cousin Annie and the bats in our living room. Cousin Annie was a Matthews and a first cousin to my grandfather, Grover. Their fathers were brothers and they lived off the highway on the next road beyond the Road to Frog Eye. Cousin Annie lived at the old home with her husband, Alfred Thompson, who was either Amish or Quaker.

Remember me telling you about Charlotte Taylor having living quarters in the feed room on the end of the chicken house? Well, Cousin Laura (so I called her) lived in a feed room at the end of the Thompson's chicken house, the end close to Cousin Annie's kitchen. I do not know why I called her Cousin Laura. I guess because everyone else who lived there was a cousin. She was a very thin older Black woman who had plats in her hair and was missing numerous teeth, but she always had a smile as big as any you've ever seen. She dressed different than the others and wore print dresses that seemed to have been the style at the time. It was probably something that Cousin Annie saw to, and I can see her in a blue-and-white print dress with a big starched white collar. Mom would pull up in the yard, and I would jump out of the car and go running to see Cousin Laura in her living quarters. She would greet me with open arms and hug me every time, and just smile, always happy to see me.

Cousin Laura's quarters were sparse, with a small table and a chair in front of the window, and there was a kerosene lamp. Her bed was the first rope bed that I had ever seen, and it had a mattress that did not cover the entire length of the bed. I would fiddle with the ropes then climb on the bed and sit there while she talked to me. Cousin Annie brought all of Laura's hot meals to her quarters and ate them on her wooden table. If I was in Cousin Annie's house, I would take Cousin Laura jars of iced tea, and I always wanted to help Cousin Annie carry her meals to her. I am not sure that I ever saw her working in the house, but maybe I did.

Cousin Annie lived in a huge old Victorian two-story house that was owned by her father, Ambrose Matthews, and her mother, Laura Darby. The house was loaded with antique furniture and had a ton of dark woodwork and doors. I remember a lace tablecloth on a huge dining room table. There was a big front porch, but the landmark was the windmill that pumped water, and it was always turning in the wind. It was one of few windmills that still stood at the time, and it could be seen from the highway. On the backside of the kitchen there was a large grape arbor and the yard was full of huge shade trees. Cousin Alfred had one of those cloth-covered beach chairs (orange and green striped) that sat under a tree, and every year the robins would build a nest in that grape arbor. You could see them from the kitchen windows, and every year I wanted to see those baby birds. I would get an old box or basket and climb on it to try and see the birds. Every time I was almost there, Cousin Alfred would yell at me to get down and leave the birds alone. One day I managed to get past him and made it, but I did not get past the mother robin. She flew into me and was pecking at my head and would not stop. I ran screaming, but Cousin Alfred just stood there and laughed. That incident may have been the end of my bird ventures.

Cousin Annie was like another grandparent, who would take me to different places with her. She took me to my first dentist appointment to get my teeth cleaned. She used to take me to Main Street in Pocomoke City when she would go to shop. She was always at church and visited often at our house. Her husband, who we called Cousin Alfred, was a thin man who wore suspenders and a big dark floppy brim hat all the time. He had a skinny beard that went almost down to his waist, and when he died, they took his body to Baltimore to be buried. I remember the conversations about a three-day celebration of his life when all they did was eat and dance.

Based on that memory, maybe he wasn't Quaker or Amish, or maybe that is how they celebrate, as he sure looked like it. I'm not sure which religion celebrates for three days, but I believe he was born and raised in Baltimore. They had one child, a son named Winfield who went to school and became a surgeon living near Raleigh, North Carolina. Mom and Dad would go to North Carolina to visit him and his wife. They lived in Goldsborough and had a daughter, Linda, whom I used to play with when we were children. I was living in Maryland when he died, and I remember Mother was so upset.

Aunt Annie Reid, my Mentor

As much as I loved spending time with Cousin Laura in her little corner of the world, it was Aunt Annie Reid whom I spent countless hours with. That was probably because she lived within walking distance of our house, as her house sat up a lane directly across from our grandfather's house. She lived with her husband, Reverend Alexander Reid, and they had three children. Reverend Reid was the preacher of Frog Eye Church just a few miles down the road from us. It was probably the only Black Congregational church in that part of the county. He was a very tall man and spoke with a heavy accent, but she was my mentor, my companion, and my teacher.

The Reids lived in a two-story house, and there was a woodshed with a flat roof beside the house. I remember that shed well, for on top of it sat a huge five-gallon glass jar, and in that jar was a giant brown snake with markings on it. I was told it belonged to their son, Alexander, who was away at school. There was some type of liquid in the jar and the snake appeared to be alive. The vision is clear, as once I got to the top of the lane, I would move as far away from the driveway as I could and away from the snake as far as possible and go in the back door. Aunt Annie had a woodstove in her kitchen, and she would be cooking. It was always warm in there as I sat at her kitchen table and watched her cook. I wonder what we talked about. On the other side of the house was the parlor with a piano and a pretty little piano stool with glass ball feet. I used to love to sit on that stool and turn round and round. Their teenage daughter, Charlotte, played the piano and she would go in there and play music for me.

Aunt Annie was always dressed in rather long dresses and kept a bandana tied on her head. She carried a long wooden pole and a burlap bag with her. We were walking out her lane one day and all of a sudden, a huge black snake came out of the weeds right in front of us. He was stretched across the entire lane and still coming. She yelled for me to get back, and I ran. She started hitting that darn snake with the pole, and that thing leaped up in the air several times her height. He slithered off somewhere and we were on our way. There was a strawberry patch on the opposite side of the lane, and she would take me there to pick strawberries. I remember one day when I stooped in that patch and got into a bed of red ants. They got into my shorts and underwear and were stinging me everywhere. Aunt Annie pulled down my clothes and was swatting ants off me right there in the field. She took me back to her house and put some kind of salve on the stings.

In the wintertime, Aunt Annie would come to get me, and she always wore gloves with the fingers worn out and carried that pole. She would scout the cut cornfields looking for turnip greens to get enough for her dinner. I thought the ones with the yellow flowers were pretty, but she did not want to eat the ones that were blooming. I would go home with her and sit there at that table, and she would crank up that old cookstove a notch, get it nice and warm, and then cook her greens and fish. She always took some to Mom and Dad. At the same time, she would be baking cornbread in the oven of that old woodstove, and it was good.

She would take me in the woods with her and and tell me what every leaf was and what tree it fell from. For years, I could identify any tree in the region because of Aunt Annie's lessons. I was in the woods one day and saw a flower blooming. It was almost totally covered with pine needles, but I could see the pink flower peeping through from under the holly tree. She told me that was a jack-in-the-pulpit, and I was in awe. We did not pull up that flower. I have only seen one other growing in the woods in my lifetime. Aunt Annie showed me how moss grows on one side of the tree, and if I ever got lost in the woods to look at the bark to find my way out. Of course, you would have to know which way you were headed, and I didn't. Roger Swift also showed me that one day in the woods, but I do not remember which side of the tree the moss grows on now.

As the holidays were getting close, Aunt Annie would take her burlap sack and go into the woods gathering holly berries and cedar for Mother to make her Christmas wreaths. She discovered crow's feet that grew on the ground and in pine needles. I remember Mother being so happy to get it as it was soft and did not prick her fingers like the cedar did. Aunt Annie would sit in the kitchen with Mom making little bouquets of those holly berries to go on the wreaths. There are only certain kinds of branches that will bend in a round circle, and Aunt Annie would go cut those branches. She and Mom would bend them and wire them together before they ever started with the wreaths. I am sure that Mother paid her for helping her with the task.

When Aunt Annie went to Frog Eye Church to dust the pews and pulpit and clean the floors, she would take me with her. Like all the old churches, the windows were stained glass, and I was in awe when the sun would shine through them, making everything glow inside that church. This had to be before I started school, since I went with her as often during cold weather as I did in the warm weather.

I lost track of Lem, Charlotte Taylor, Cousin Laura and Aunt Annie when I moved away, but when I started writing about them, I wanted to know who they really were, that they could leave such an impression on a young child's heart. Now I know....

I could not find anything about Lem in the 1940 census. He was not living on Buddy Price's property according to the census taker. Charlotte Taylor was only twenty in the census. I learned that she was single, worked as a servant in a private home, and rented the property wherever she lived. She attended two years of school. I find no other records of her, which probably means that she married, and her name changed.

The Reid story is interesting. Reverend Alexander Reid was born in the West Indies in 1886, as were both of his parents. That explains his heavy accent that made him hard to understand. He was a minister who had immigrated to the United States in 1906 when he was twenty years old, and the census shows him moving around for the ME Church. Aunt Annie was born in Maryland in 1890 as Annie Lydia Barkley. She had attended college. She and Reverend Reid had three children: Alexander, George, and Charlotte. Alexander registered in the WWII draft and his application shows that he was fifty-eight years old, born in Jamaica, and worked as a Methodist minister. He died in 1968, and she lived until 1979.

Someone sent me a newspaper article about Charlotte and the story of Frog Eye Church, so I was able to contact her through the church. She had married a Rolly and lived on the back road to Pocomoke. She remembered who I was and said there was an old photo in the album of me standing by her piano. She said that her daddy had an old Model A that my daddy used to keep running for him. I told her the story about Charlie Smith and that he was buried at the church when I was a baby, and I was looking for his tombstone. She said there is not one there for him. We had a nice conversation, and I told her I would call her on my next trip to the shore. I intended to get the photo, but never did.

But the story that makes my heart sing is the story of Cousin Laura. The only family she had were the Thompsons. In the 1910 Census, I found her living in Accomack, Virginia with her brother, Noah, his wife, four of his children, her mother Harriet Hargis, age sixty-one, and two of Laura's sisters. They all were laborers on a farm. The next time I find her mentioned is in the 1940 Census living on Cousin Annie and Alfred Thompson's property around the corner from our grandfather, Grover. Remember that Annie, Addie, and Grover were first cousins. She is listed as Laura Hargis, age forty-six, single and working as a servant in a private home. She has never attended school and was born in Virginia.

I located a record where Laura applied for Social Security benefits in 1966 and her residence is listed as Goldsborough, North Carolina. Bingo! I stumbled on her death certificate, and she passed away on December 25, 1972. The attending physician was Winfield Thompson, and the informant on the death certificate was his wife, Louise (Cousin Annie's son and daughter-in-law). The certificate states that she was born on July 2, 1892 in Virginia. So that skinny little Black woman who used to smile with all those missing teeth and open her arms wide when I went running to her had moved to North Carolina when Cousin Annie moved in with her son, the doctor, and his family after Cousin Alfred died. That little woman had never attended the first day of school and used to work as a farm laborer. The little woman who wore the ironed print dresses with the starched white collars, the one with the contagious smile and missing teeth, had lived to be eighty years old. Good for the Thompsons and good for Laura Hargis, as they did not leave her behind! There's not a doubt in my mind that the Thompsons treated her like family. This discovery made me feel good about the human race and the members of our family.

My thoughts are that she was probably a descendant of slaves in Virginia, but I could not trace her family back that far. I did, however, find a large White family living there by the name of Hargis that were farmers. If I could have devoted more time to the search, I am sure that my suspicions could be proven that Cousin Laura descended from slaves who were once owned by the wealthy Hargis family.

Joyce Matthews
Third Grade

OUR PETS

The first pet I remember having was a big German Shepherd whose name was Pal. I do not know where the dog came from or when I got him, as I was young. Pal stayed close to me, and we would play for hours. Daddy had a fifty-five-gallon oil drum at the house, and I would roll that drum to the front yard, climb on it with my bare feet, and try to walk it from one end of the yard to the other without falling off. I remember the struggle of trying to reach that goal until finally I could do it, turn around, and go the other direction without falling. Pal would get so excited and run and bark as I maneuvered that thing with my feet. Somewhere along the way, I found a long stick and an old tin bucket. I would carry the stick rattling that bucket and Pal would walk on his hind feet beside me on the barrel. We did this every day and when I started school, Pal and I would do it when I got home. Maybe I was aiming for the circus.... Once, Pal went missing, and Daddy looked for him for days, maybe weeks. Either someone found him, or I heard them saying that Pal died after getting caught in a muskrat trap down at Do Right Price's marsh, and that the trap was deliberately set to get him. I know I was lost without him and cried my eyes out over Pal.

A woman named Leonia Revell (my fifth-grade teacher later) heard about my loss and offered Mother a collie puppy. I got that baby, and he was so cute. I named him Laddie, as Lassie was big at the time. Laddie is the one that ate my chocolate chicken on Easter night. Laddie would run out in the road, so I did not have him long before he got killed by a car.

I think it was a while before I had another dog, as I used to walk that road with my next one. He was a Blue Tick hounddog with long legs, a white birddog with black spots. I don't know for sure, but I think he came from Pop-Pop Grover's house. His name was Jack, and he went everywhere that I went in the neighborhood. One summer, Jack and I were walking home when Jack started acting funny. We were almost home, and instead of staying with me, he ran a ways down Earl Price's lane. I ran after him, trying to catch him and he started foaming from the mouth. He fell into that big irrigation ditch, and I tried to get him out, but I could not reach him. The ditch was covered in green slime, so I ran home as fast as I could and told Daddy that Jack had foam coming out of his mouth and that he had fallen in the ditch. Daddy grabbed his shotgun and took off on foot. It turned out that Jack had rabies, and Daddy had to kill him.

The last dog I had I must have gotten when I was about ten or so. We had been to North Carolina and Mother's Aunt Maggie (Granddaddy Alex Jones' half sister and Uncle Fred Brothers' wife). Uncle Fred was a favorite when we went to North Carolina, and he used to take me to his grape arbor to pick scuppernong grapes, and I loved them. They had an old general store in the front yard, and there were purple lizards running everywhere, which I did not like. On this visit, his dog had a litter of puppies. They looked like border collies. He gave me a little female, and I named her Suzie. When we were coming home on the ferry that day, Daddy and I went to the car to get the puppy. She went running on the lower deck of the ferry and ran beyond the rope where no one was allowed to go. Of course, I was terrified that she was going to end up in the bay, but some man who worked on the ferry crossed the rope and rescued her. Suzie lived for a long time, and there was a photo of me sitting in the yard with Suzie when I was a teenager. I do not remember Suzie's fate.

I had a baby-blue parakeet that was probably inspired by the one that belonged to Aunt Agnes and Mom-Mom Amy. We kept the parakeet on the screened-in porch during the warm months, and one day, a bad storm was moving in. Mom brought the birdcage inside and set it next to the kitchen sink. As fate would have it, lightning hit the water pipe at the sink. The poor parakeet started squawking and tossing around in the cage with feathers flying everywhere. In a split second my parakeet was fried.

Wayne and I both had a pet rabbits, and my favorite was a big white rabbit with black spots that had little pink babies. Daddy had an overflow of rabbits that did not fit in the barn at Buddy Price's house, so the overflow of rabbits lived in pens in our yard. Every day when Wayne and I got home from school, we had to feed and water the rabbits in those pens. I recall that in the wintertime the water in their bowls would freeze, and we would have to break the ice out of the bowls to refill them. It was Hurricane Hazel that took all of the rabbits that lived in the pens. The rabbits, pens, and everything else blew away in the hurricane. After that, there was a lot of chatter about the tame rabbits breeding with the wild ones in the area.

Then there was Wayne's pig, Porky. He was fat and white with black spots. Porky gets his own paragraph in the chapter, "Storm Memories."

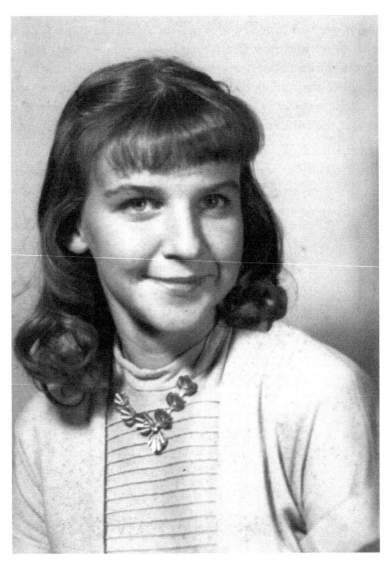

Joyce Matthews
(No date)

THE GREAT WHITE HUNTERS

Daddy and Pop-Pop did a lot of hunting and would return with squirrels, rabbits, and quail. They would nail them up on the back of our shed to skin and clean them, probably because of all the dogs at Pop-Pop's house. Pop-Pop Grover raised dogs and had a lot of them. They were all hunting dogs, beagles or bird dogs, and I remember him standing at his back door many times throwing last night's biscuits out the door to those dogs one at a time. Maybe they cooked extra for the dogs. I doubt he bought dog food if there was such a thing then.

I don't know where they came from, but one night Daddy and I were at Pop-Pop and Edna's house when she was cooking eel. Edna had a large pan of eel on that hot woodstove, and she was trying to hold the lid on the pan. Those green slimy things were jumping out of the pan all over the top of the hot stove. I guess she finally got them under control and cooked them. I did not like the looks of those things. They had a huge cat named Boogie that was the size of a bobcat. Boogie was so big that he could see over the table when he put his front paws on it. Boogie was beside himself that night trying to get to the eel. It was said that he was seventeen years old at the time.

I remember seeing all the quail nailed up on the shed and Mother fussing about how small they were and how many it would take to feed everybody. Quail were plentiful at the time, and you could always hear the "bob, bob white" or the "whipporwill" songs. Mother did not like the squirrel or rabbit meat, and she complained about how tough and dry it was. She was a happy camper when Daddy and his business partner started raising chinchillas and tame rabbits. The partner's wife gave Mother a recipe for a tame-rabbit dish that was fantastic. All I remember was that, after she dredged it in flour and salt, she added milk and baked it in the oven and she would make it on Sundays. I used to love visiting the business partner's house with Mom and Dad because his wife had collected antique glass buttons and had them all framed and hanging on one living room wall. She also had a large crock sitting on a living room table filled with cattails. It caught my attention since the only place I had ever seen them was in the ditches.

Along the way, Daddy got into frog gigging at the irrigation pond near our house. He had a gigger and would take his flashlight out at night and come home with great big frogs. After they were skinned, the legs looked like chicken legs when Mother cooked them, and I remember that she liked them. Finally, the day came when I was old enough to go gigging with Daddy, and it was a sight to behold. Once you reached the irrigation pond, the frogs would get quiet. Then you would move the flashlight around the pond and see all these eyes staring at you. Hundreds of red eyes glaring in the dark. The gigger was on a long handle so you could stab them with the little pitch fork on the end and get them in a bag. I bought a gigger here at a yard sale in Deltaville years ago, just for a keepsake. Later, someone stole my frog gigger out of the garage.

Then came deer-hunting season. To my knowledge, Grover never hunted deer. Therefore, Daddy had never hunted them, but he decided he was going to get a deer. He left home early that morning headed to Kingston, I believe. He said he didn't see a deer, and finally got tired of looking, so he sat down near a tree to rest. He fell asleep, but something woke him, and when he opened his eyes, there was a deer staring him down. He said he looked at that deer's big brown eyes and wondered how anyone could kill something so pretty. He came home with his gun and his story and never went deer hunting again.

The Storms

We always had a lot of electric storms as they followed the rivers and creeks and would keep circling around and coming back. I hated the storms, especially when Mom and Dad were both working, and I was home with the younger kids. I remember standing at the kitchen door connected to the porch and watching bolts of lightning streak through the sky on the other side of the cornfields. I would just shake in horror, as I knew it was coming our way.

Mother had told the story often that when I was a toddler and the house was still sitting at the edge of the woods, a bad storm moved in. She had closed all the windows except the kitchen window that she left partially open. I was sitting in my highchair eating when a bolt of lightning entered that window and went around and around the baseboards and then hit my highchair and knocked the spoon out of my hand. I have often wondered if that is where my fear of storms began. Perhaps it was a blessing that I was in the highchair, as Aunt Agnes had told me that I had a wooden playpen where I stayed most of the time. She went on to say that Mother was not one to sit around and hold her babies all day and that once we were fed and dressed, we went in the playpen until lunchtime, and then until dinner since Mother was a busy woman.

When I was a little older, I was at Pop-Pop Grover's house playing with Mary Jo when a storm started rolling in. I jumped on my bike and high- tailed it home, looking over my shoulder trying to figure out how close those lightning bolts were behind me. All of a sudden, there was Earl Price coming out his lane in his Studebaker, and he pretended that he was going to run over me. I swerved my bike in the gravel on the side of the road and went head-on into the irrigation ditch. The ditch was covered in green slime and there were muskrats swimming everywhere. There I was in the ditch with them and it was lightning and thundering and Earl Price was laughing. I feared that I was going to get bitten by a muskrat before the lightning got me. Oh, God, I was angry at that grown man and his childish prank. He could have tried to help me out of the ditch! I was covered in slime and more than likely resembled the green hulk with all that mess dripping off me.

We had some rather heavy snow storms also and obviously it got really cold. That same spot in the irrigation ditch, where the T was a favorite spot for a hut was cold and the ditch had frozen over. The frozen brush weighed down with snow covered the ditch, and a bunch of us kids could sit under it on the ice out of sight. All kids had snowsuits with heavy pants and coats. I had a pink snowsuit and Wayne had a navy-blue one. Still, we would come home frozen, and many times Mom would have made rice pudding. She also made us snowcream when it snowed, but not on the first snow because "that had all the germs in it."

Then there were the storms that brought flooding in the low-lying areas of Somerset County. When there were warnings, Mom and Dad would take us to their friend's house, Red and Beatrice Renshaw, in Fruitland, just outside of Princess Anne where we would stay. It was after one of those storms that they came back to check on things and there was probably still a foot or so of standing water. The old outhouse was still standing in the corner of the yard, so this was before the addition. During the storm, the door to the outhouse had come off and was floating in the water. Wayne and I found some sticks, poles, or something and climbed on that toilet door, and with those sticks, we were able to paddle all over that place on our raft. Huckleberry Finn would have been jealous, and it is a wonder we didn't contract a deadly disease.

Somewhere along the way, Daddy and Pop-Pop had put pigs in the woods across the road from the house, and that is where Wayne's pig, Porky, lived. Porky was a fat white pig with black spots. Again, we came home to check on things and the water was high, but now I know that there must have been a high tide expected. I know that because Daddy brought Porky out of the woods and somehow got the pig onto Mother's screened porch. We left again, and I remember the day we came home, and

Mother fussing and being very upset because there were piles of pig poop and mud everywhere on her screened porch. I think that's when Porky went to market. Maybe Wayne remembers for sure.

Then there was the storm of all storms during our childhood on October 24, 1954. Hurricane Hazel came up the east coast when I was eleven years old. Wayne would have been six, Phyllis three, and Glen just a year-and-a half. Daddy was working in Pocomoke City, and he was driving a black car which may have been his 1949 Plymouth. I remember Mom's anxiety that day, waiting for him to get home before the hurricane hit the area. I remember somebody trying to get Pop-Pop, Edna, and the kids to come to our house, but he would not budge. Pop-Pop had a construction company there at the house for days jacking up the house to put a new foundation under it. They had gotten word at noontime that the hurricane was going to slam Somerset County. They threw their tools in the back of the truck and left, making no effort to tie down the house.

So the story goes, when the contractors left, Pop-Pop Grover went upstairs and crawled in bed and would not leave to come to our house. He was lying there in his bed listening to the wind blow. When he saw the mirror swinging back and forth on the dresser, he went downstairs and told Edna to gather up the kids, Mary Jo and Allen, as it was time to go. So, some hours into the storm, later that afternoon, they came to our house during the worst wind and rain.

Mother had two windows over the kitchen sink and every few minutes Pop-Pop would get up and look out those windows checking on the old house across the field. I have no idea what the time span was nor how many trips he made to that window, but I do remember his words to this day, "Well Edna, she's gone." Of course, everyone wanted to look out of those two small windows, but no one could leave the house to go check on anything. The storm had picked up the house and turned the top floor in one direction and the bottom floor in a different direction and then just plopped it down. He and Daddy went there later that night with flashlights, and Mary Jo and I watched the lights from the bedroom window. Mother had a daybed that was used when overnight guests came to visit. Mary Jo and I both slept on that narrow single bed for a few weeks after the hurricane went through, and I remember the arguments between us as she slept at one end and me at the other. The complaint was that there was nowhere to put her legs, so I assume my long legs were in her way.

We will never know how many family heirlooms were lost that day, but there was a Victorian fainting couch in an upstairs bedroom, and I remember seeing them throw that over the hill into the woods, like they did with wagons loaded with stuff. I went there every day with Daddy, as he was on a mission. His mission was to find his grandmother Jo's lamp, and he finally did. Defying all odds, neither piece was broken in that pile of rubble. It was sometime after Pop-Pop's death that Edna gave the lamp to Daddy on one of his trips to the shore. Edna also gave him the mantel clock and Mary Jo was under the impression that he got the family Bible. He did not, and we have no clue whatever happened to it, unless it went over the hill also.

I brought the lamp here on Halloween night in 2005 shortly after Mother's death in fear that someone would break into her house and break or steal the lamp. I still have it here on a washstand beside my bed. That means the lamp has only been moved twice since Grandmom Jo bought it in 1906. It lived up to the name, Hurricane Lamp. Steve says that he remembers sitting there watching Daddy electrify the old oil lamp, when he brought it to Virginia.

Not only were most of their belongings lost, but Daddy and his partner that were in the rabbit business lost most of the rabbits. They used to raise chinchilla rabbits and regular rabbits and sell them to restaurants in the city for gourmet cooks. Not only did they lose the four rows of rabbit cages at our house with rabbits on both sides—probably forty—but they also rented a barn from Buddy Price that was loaded with chinchilla rabbits. I think they may have recovered a few, but Hurricane Hazel took out most of the old barn. So, Wayne and I lost our pet rabbits, too. Looking back, I realize none of our pets fared well.

Pop-Pop and Edna made temporary living quarters in the old smokehouse for them and their children. It was cramped with two iron beds, a table and chairs, and a stove of some type for heating and cooking. They were hunkered down safe and warm and spent at least one Christmas in that smokehouse with Mary Jo and Allen. I remember a small cedar tree sitting there with Mary Jo's paper chains on it. Finally, a four- or-five-room home was built where the old house had set, and it seemed to take forever to get it completed with all the delays and snags along the way.

Summers Spent on The Road to Frog Eye

The only store in the area was Lawrence Burgess' store on the corner of the main road, and Daddy would take us to the store every now and then. The counter was loaded with penny candy and a big round of cheddar cheese. They would cut you a slab of cheese, wrap it in brown paper, and tie it with a string. Daddy was a cheese lover all his life, and I would look at the Mary Jane shoes and baseball bats and ask for a banana every time. I remember the Burgess family trying to convince me that I wanted candy or ice cream, but I never wavered from the bananas. Besides that, I saved my ice cream adventures for the ice cream truck that came by Mom-Mom Amy and Aunt Agnes' house every day that I was there. I loved the sound of the dinging bell on the truck, as that was not something country kids were privy to.

We spent most of our time on Roger and Myrtle Swift's farm when we were very young, but then we spent just as much time on Pop-Pop Grover's farm when we were older, and there were more of us.

Everyone had their own bike, and it appears that Glen had a tractor, according to photographs. Mary Jo and I kept busy outdoors on the farm running through those cornfields, and it is a miracle that we did not get bitten by a snake. I admired the morning glories that opened early in the day on those cornstalks and thought they were so pretty. They were vibrant colors of pink, purple, and some white. I would catch glimpses of them in all the cornfields when riding the bus to school. I still see them growing here and there in the cornfields and remember those on the Matthews farm. Somebody planted and grew tomatoes out there also. Sometimes instead of having an egg sandwich for lunch, as there was always a bowl full on the kitchen table at their house, she and I would take her mother's saltshaker to the tomato patch and sit there eating tomatoes. In the fall, there were round pears on the tree, and they were so good, maybe better than the tomatoes. Mary Jo reminded me that they were called sickle pears.

Their house had two staircases, one on each end, and a third one that went to the attic. Mary Jo and I would go up the one that had two small rooms just off to the left. One of those rooms had a lot of stuff stored in it, and I don't think we were supposed to be in there. In a box, Mary Jo found her mother's breast pump. She must have watched Edna use it because she knew that if we put it on our boobies and squeezed something would happen. We thought we would get boobs, I guess. We squeezed it a lot, but nothing happened. There was also a wooden trunk-like box that was loaded with little white porcelain child's dishes. We were not allowed to play with them either, but we did. There were tons of dishes in that trunk, and I now believe they belonged to Pop-Pop Grover's sister, Ada Florence, who died when she was about five years old. I confirmed this when I started researching the family.

In the large bedroom upstairs, there was a lot of big antique furniture. There were also a lot of quilts, and Edna would hang them out the upstairs windows to air them out. Maybe they were getting peed on at night by the kids.

It wasn't all fun and games there either, as we had to work in the heat of the summer. Pop-Pop Grover raised chickens, and for the most part, they were fryers. This means they were raised from biddies in his chicken houses and sent to market at an early age. The chicken houses were hot, and they stunk inside, but every chicken had to be caught on the leg with this long metal rod that had a loop on the end. Once you caught the chicken, Pop-pop would stick this capsule down its throat and put a colored band around the chicken's leg to let you know it had been given the medication. The disease was called coccidiosis that you were trying to avoid. I do not remember what he had Mary Jo and I doing but we did a lot of it, all day long in the hot stinking chicken house. The laying hens were also given a handful of crushed oyster shells in their feeders to help increase the density of the eggshells.

In the feed room there was a corn sheller that was cranked by hand, and we had to feed the corn sheller one ear at a time while one turned the crank to shell the corn for the animals. We toted buckets of water for him to pour into the chicken's water fountains. I'm not sure why, but Daddy fed and watered the chickens in the evening, and Mother must have been working her nighttime nursing job, as he would take me with him to feed the chickens.

When Daddy walked into the feed room, he would make me stand by the door until he turned on a dim lightbulb. Then he shone the flashlight around the rafters looking for snakes. It was right there that I saw my first snake, a black snake stretched out on the rafter. Daddy said many times that mice were attracted to the chicken feed, which in turn attracted the snakes to eat the mice. There were metal coal shuttles (buckets) that were used for the chicken feed, and when Daddy moved to Virginia, he brought one of them with him. He gave me that bucket many, many years ago and I painted it and put an eagle decal on it for a magazine bucket. I still have it here in the shed.

Years after Pop-Pop Grover died, I decided that I wanted that old wooden cornsheller to set in my living room. When I asked Mary Jo about the cornsheller, she said that our grandfather had sold all the old farm equipment to Lawrence Burgess who intended to open a museum right there where his grocery store sat. When I inquired, as I was willing to pay for it, I learned that *American Pickers* had been in there and bought all of the old farm inventory that had been collected for the local museum. So there went the cornsheller that we had spent so many summers cranking in that stinking-hot chicken house.

Our grandfather raised fryer chickens. The little baby yellow biddies would come in on the train by the hundreds in large cardboard boxes with little air holes cut in the them. They would be peeping and so cute, but he only raised them for six weeks, and off to market they went. In a couple weeks they would be running around naked. Then, all of a sudden, their white feathers started appearing, but they appeared half naked, which was their ugly stage. It was crucial to get them shipped out in a timely manner or they would not have been tender. Mother was a fan of young fryers and got to the point she would not buy chickens from the store. Pop-pop also had laying hens that lived in the back chicken house. There was always a bowl of fresh eggs sitting on their table. For some reason all of his chickens were white. When I was traveling back and forth to Maryland, I would see a truck loaded with crates of chickens and actually felt sorry for them, as I knew where they were headed.

On the days that we were not in the chicken house with him, we were riding on the cultivator behind his tractor. I guess the horses and handplow had been retired. He had acres of newly planted corn, and he would cultivate it to keep the weeds out until it grew to a certain height. We started out having to walk behind that thing and would uncover a plug of corn if it got covered with a glob of dirt by the cultivator. Eventually, Mary Jo and I were old enough that we could ride on the back of that thing, jump off when necessary, and jump back on. That was a good day. I remember the times that he would holler and fuss at us, which he did often.

I might have been going through a growth spurt and one day when I went to Pop-Pop's house to play, he looked at me and asked why I had bothered to even put on those shorts. I was puzzled and did not understand what he meant, so I asked. He yelled, "Why don't you just take them off, so we can look at your ass all day?" It took me a long time to even comprehend what he meant, but I was crushed. I doubt that I was even eight or nine years old. That is how our paternal grandfather was, and that is how I remember him.

Pop-Pop also had at least three horses in the pasture when I was a kid. It seemed that two of them were younger and maybe there was one old mule. Mary Jo informed me that they were all mules, whatever a mule is. I know the young ones were shiny black and named King and Queen and they were majestic looking. Daddy used to ride them, and there was a photo of him as a young man sitting on one of those horses, a great picture. It went by the wayside just like all the other family photos.

In the middle of the field on the left there was a growth of tall trees, like a big circle of them, and it was referred to as the graveyard. Pop-pop was always yelling and reminding us kids to stay away from the graveyard and he plowed away from all those trees. I am still trying to reach a conclusion about who is buried in that graveyard on the Matthews farm.

About five years ago, I joined a Somerset County group and put out the word looking for pictures of the old house or pictures taken after

Hurricane Hazel went through there. I did not get a picture, but a woman answered that she drove by there every day and the tombstone that used to set on the hill was now gone. We never saw a tombstone there, but obviously when the property was sold for lots, the field was cleared of the trees. I assume Edna sold it off, as Allen still lives there. The woman told me there had been a tombstone there on the hill for years beside a pine tree. No one knew what was written on the stone, and the man who owned the first lot had done away with it. I left a message for Allen to call me, but never heard back from him, so I do not know if Pop-Pop Grover's sister, Ada Florence, was buried there or Mom-Mom Amy's baby, but I do know that he was protective of the area. I am going to look into dates of Ada Florence's death compared to when they bought the old farm, which may answer the question.

On Sunday afternoons, we would take a ride and sometimes go to Crisfield, or Mom and Dad would take us to a place called Coulbourne's Creek where we could swim. I was playing near the shore, as I feared the deep water. There was this heavy-set, red-headed woman from Crisfield who pushed me under and sat on me. I was convinced I was drowning and that experience created my fear of the water. I knew that woman's name for years but now only remember her first name, Irene. I hated her from that day on.

Mother and Daddy had numerous friends that lived in Crisfield and one couple was Lorraine Smith and her husband called "Smitty." They had a daughter named Llewellyn that was shorter than I was. Consequently, mother passed down all my outgrown clothes to her. I remember clearly when they would visit us, and Mother and Lorraine would go through my clothes. Mother would give away skirts and dresses that I loved, and I would get so upset with her. We went to visit them a lot on weekends, too, when they lived on Chesapeake Avenue in Crisfield. We went there late one afternoon, and she and I were told that we needed to play outside and to not go in the living room. Of course, being kids, we were going to find out why the living room was off limits as we had sat and played in that room many times because of the mosquitoes outside. I suppose when Llewellyn thought the coast was clear, we sneaked in the front door and went in that room. There were two floorlamps lit in there and they made the entire room look pink, and there were pretty flowers everywhere. We stopped in our tracks. Why was her grandmother sleeping in a long box? Where did she get that pretty pillow? We were too young to understand what we were seeing for the first time in our young lives.

Rehobeth Baptist Church

The majority of our social life was through the church. Rehobeth Baptist Church was not far away, and our great-grandparents, George A Matthews and Josephine Darby Matthews are buried there in the family plot, as is Pop-Pop Grover and Cousin Annie's niece, Pennington, who died when she was a baby. She would have been Ambrose Matthews' grandchild. They are in one of the many Matthews plots, the first plot to the right of the front door. There used to be a wrought iron border fence around the plot but it is long gone, and only the corner markers remain. It's likely the fence was removed to allow a lawn mower in there.

Mother is the one who kept us in the church, and I remember as a child, begging Daddy to go to church with us every Sunday. He used to say that he was just as good as the guy who went to church and then came home and hung his religion up in the closet until the following Sunday. I never understood what he was saying until I was older. He was totally against the Catholic religion and preached often how the Catholics sinned all week, went to confession on Sunday, and all was forgiven. Yet, he had numerous Catholic friends in Baltimore City and had attended the churches there with them.

Ironically, that was the only place I was allowed to go for the majority of my childhood, and for some reason, Dad never got involved with a church when I was a child. That came later and he might have been a deacon and a Sunday school teacher at Rehobeth Baptist Church before they moved to Virginia. Once he moved to Virginia and started teaching Sunday school, it was all "Hail Mary" with him, to the point that we, as adults, could not even take a bottle of wine in the house in Syringa at Christmas time. I do know that they started out at Harmony Grove and from there moved to Springhill Baptist Church in Cobbs Creek. I am told that there is still a sign on one of the doors that says, "Lake Matthews' Sunday school class."

Nevertheless, Mother was active in many things at the church. We were in Sunday school every Sunday morning, and, when old enough, we sat through preaching and listened to all the hellfire-and-damnation sermons. All the kids looked forward to Vacation Bible School in the summer months, and it was held in the mornings. I remember we learned to sing "Twinkle, Twinkle Little Star" and "Jesus Loves Me." It was Mother, like all mothers, who taught me how to recite the child's prayer, "Now I Lay Me Down to Sleep," and the line about "if I should die before I wake," scared me, as I did not want to die. Everyone said grace before meals no matter whose table you sat at.

Rehobeth Baptist Church - Bible School
Phyllis is on the far left standing in front of Marie Adams.
Wayne is 4th from left (white shirt) hold his hand on his head.
Joyce is the the right on the pole on the left with long hair.

There was a group called the Girl's Auxiliary or GAs for short. Mother was the GA leader for years, and it included all the teenage girls in the church.

They would meet at different houses or at the church at times. I recall one of the meetings at our house, and they always served refreshments when the meeting was over. Mother had piled a large glass bowl with fresh fruit, and I wanted to take it to the living room for them. When I walked through the door with the bowl of fruit, they all jumped up and screamed and scared me so bad that I dropped the bowl and broke it.

Another time we were at the church for one of their meetings and afterward they decided to go outside in the graveyard to play hide-and-seek in the. It was pitch dark out there, and they all got down and looked in this hole at the end of a grave. They said they could see a skeleton in that hole, so I wanted to see it, too. I finally got my turn to look in the hole, and when I did, they all took off running and left me there. They were a lot older than me and were being typical teens. I was terrified out there in that dark graveyard by myself.

The GAs had a summer camp, and the boys had a Baptist camp that they attended in the summertime also. I always wanted to go to summer camp, but I guess there was never enough money to send me. My first boyfriend was the preacher's son and his name was Kenneth Stouffer. Kenny went to camp one summer and made me a yellow-and-green bracelet. It was plated out of some plastic material, and when he returned, he rode his bicycle from Rehobeth all the way to our house to bring me the bracelet. I remember that morning to this day when Kenneth showed up. We must have been all of nine or ten.

There were family church picnics every year, and a favorite spot was a place called Sandy Hill. We would cross a ferry with the vehicle to get to the island. They would load up Buddy Price's truck (the same one that transported the migrant workers and the same truck that almost killed Wayne and me) with hay bales for everybody to sit on and all the women would cook food for the picnic. Mother must have been the master when it came to fried chicken and deviled eggs, and that is what she always cooked for the picnics. One year we started on our journey for the picnic, and it poured so bad, we had to turn around and come back home. Everybody went to our house and we had our picnic there. We had a few church picnics at Mother's friend Hazel Wilkin's house just across the field from the church. I remember because my favorite drink was a Grapette when I was a kid, and Hazel's husband always made sure there were Grapettes buried in that tub of ice for me.

Not only did we have summer picnics, there were family dinners held inside the church once the addition was built, as the addition included a kitchen and a social area. At Halloween, I remember the event for the younger people where they would dim the lights and tell ghost stories. It was a lot of fun. One year at the family dinner they served crabcakes, crabs, and homemade ice cream. The people who had eaten the crabs and ice cream got very sick. I have never forgotten and still do not mix the two.

In addition to the Sunday school classes, kitchen, and social area, there was a new baptismal pool built behind the pulpit. Before that, the congregation would go down to the Pocomoke River in Rehobeth to baptize people in the river. I wanted no part of that scenario. There was a picture of Christ standing in the river painted on the back wall. I was eleven years old and the first one to be baptized in that pool by Reverend Bland Taylor. The same Reverend Taylor who had a home in Hartfield with his wife Bessie, which is how my parents ended up in Virginia.

The Taylors had one daughter, June, who had married and lived on the Eastern Shore. After the Taylors retired and moved back to their home

MAY 1958
Phyllis Clair Matthews (7 years old)
Glen I. Matthews (5 years old)
June Taylor's Wedding

here, June and I went to visit them on the Greyhound Bus. She had a toddler named Steve and so did I. We stayed for a week, and I fell in love with the place, as this area was so much prettier than the low-lying mud hole on the Eastern Shore.

June Taylor had married Donnie Byrd in May 1958 in Rehobeth Baptist Church. Phyllis was her flower girl and Glen was the ring bearer, so they were seven and five years old at that time. June's mother, Bessie, made her wedding gown and all the dresses for the bridesmaids. They were in a soft pastel aqua and we have a few pictures. The only pictures in our small collection of black-and-whites are of the inside of the church.

We came across the Piankatank River Bridge on that Greyhound bus and there was a white fence with yellow roses blooming everywhere, not to mention all the flowers that Mrs. Taylor had growing. I stayed a week and talked to Daddy on the phone and told him that he and Mom needed to move there. Reverend Taylor helped him find a job at Fleet Brothers in Hartfield, and they moved to Virginia in April 1960, shortly after my visit to the Taylor's home.

Jerry got out of the Navy and found a job working for Coca Cola on Main Street in Gloucester County, and we rented a little bungalow in Hartfield. Terrie was a baby and sleeping in a crib but we were not there long before moving back to Crisfield. He finally got a call to go to work at the Newport News Shipbuilding and Dry Dock. When Timley was a little over two, I moved back home to my parents' house with my three children. The rest is history.

Back to the church, I was allowed to go to the Bible studies, choir practices, the Sunday sermons and anything else, as long as it was associated with the church, per my Daddy, and God help me if there was a revival. For those of you who were not brought up in the Southern Baptist Church and not familiar with the summer revivals, let me educate you. I am not sure how far they go back, but I know they had them on Smith Island back in the 1800s. They might go way back to the preachers that used to travel from place to place on horseback.

In our neck of the woods, a preacher from another area would come to the church and he would preach every night for one to two weeks. As the guest preacher, while he was there, he and his family had to be fed lunch and dinner every day. Yes, Mother would take her turn cooking for them, and I remember the kids having to sit on the sidelines on that daybed until the adults ate their meal. Mother would fry chicken, and I would sit there in agony praying that the preacher and his wife and kids would not eat it all the chicken legs. Mom had made her famous lemon meringue pies for one of the preachers and his family and while they were eating lunch, I decided to help her by getting the pie out of the refrigerator. When I pulled it out of the fridge, I dumped it upside down in the floor. No doubt, I made her day with that trick.

If you wanted to get out of the house and go see your friends, the revival was the place to go...that is, if you could stay quiet for hours, depending on the preacher. The first time I was allowed to go anywhere with a boy was the night my parents let me go to a revival in Chincoteague, Virginia with the deacon's son, Ellsworth Hall Jr. It was a night to remember, as, first of all, I sat so far on the other side of the front seat of the car, afraid he was going to touch me, it is a wonder the door didn't fly open. I wore a red taffeta dress with several starched crinolines and little black slingbacks that I remember well. Why do I remember my outfit? Because the revival was in a tent, and it was hot as hell and the mosquitoes had no mercy. They ate up my feet, legs, and arms and got hung up under those starched netted crinolines, and obviously could not escape. I was squirming all the way home digging my feet, legs and everything else that I could reach. It was apparent that Chincoteague had as many mosquitoes as Crisfield—maybe more. I don't think Ellsworth ever asked me to go anywhere with him again.

It was Ellsworth's sister, Helen Hall, with whom I spent a lot of Sunday afternoons. She lived down on Marumsco Creek, and her father was a deacon at the church. I would go home with her and her family when church was over, and we would eat dinner then help her mother clean up the dishes and gather up the chicken bones. Helen was going to teach me how to crab with a chicken bone and string, and teach me she did. It is a miracle that we were never bitten by a water snake, as we were all over that marshland barefooted and catching crabs. It was a struggle to give up the fun, get back in time to eat, change clothes, and make it back to the Sunday-evening service, but that is how it was done. I may have been twelve or so at the time and I loved it, just as I loved crabbing in Middlesex County when my children were little, and then with my grandchildren. We even took Jennifer crabbing with us a few times. I recently learned that Ellsworth Hall Jr has been gone for years, but that his sister Helen still resides in Crisfield.

In addition to social gatherings at the church, they were also held at the parsonage down in the little village of Rehobeth. Just a hop, skip, and jump from the church. The house was always pretty, and there would be a punch bowl and cake for dessert when we went there for the socials. The kids were allowed to go out and run around the neighborhood and through the old cemeteries there.

I went back to Rehobeth Baptist Church several times and took Steven Dale when he was a toddler. At the last service I attended, the pianist, Gladys Mae and the organist (older woman) got into a shouting match up near the pulpit over who was going to play for the Sunday service. This happened before church ever started. In the end, the older woman played the organ and Gladys Mae played the piano, so I guess neither of them won that battle.

When I go to the Eastern Shore, I always stop in the churchyard and visit the Matthews plot. I was there in 2015 and left a ceramic vase full of pansies at the foot of Grandmom Jo's grave and told her I was grateful to her for raising my dad. She is buried between George and Grover. The bushes around the church were overgrown and the trim was coming off the vestibule. It was sad-looking and the worst I had ever seen it. Some old people in the county told me that the population had aged or died off and there was no one to keep up the church or the grounds anymore. The cemetery is loaded with tombstones that read Matthews, and I researched all them a couple years ago. I was not surprised that the majority of them are our Matthews family members through one lineage or another, and I think there was only one Matthews couple there that we were not related to.

This past spring in 2022 someone put out a plea for donations to help maintain the church cemetery. They were looking for descendants of those who are buried there, as indeed many of the families are deceased or had moved from the area years ago. A woman whom I am friends with on Facebook had been raised in the church and she notified me of the fund drive. I was put it touch with the gentleman who was handling the account and in turn notified Phyllis and a cousin, Sandra Matthews Marshall. Phyllis and I both donated money toward maintaining the grounds this past year. Sandra, in turn, notified another cousin and everyone did their part. The drive was very successful.

WE MOVED TO POCOMOKE CITY

We moved to Pocomoke City I am guessing because Daddy got a job there as a mechanic, although it was not that far from where we lived. We moved to 309 Linden Avenue to a large old Victorian home that had a lot more rooms than were in our other house. There was a back stairs, and a front stairs, and Mom would fuss when Wayne and I would run up one and come down the other. There was a summer sleeping porch upstairs with windows all down one side of the room. That's where our toys were. It was a beautiful home compared to the old farmhouse we were used to living in.

I remember Phyllis, with her long dark curls, scooting from room to room on the hardwood floor with that leg stuck out instead of crawling. It must have been summer because she was only in a diaper. There was a large kitchen with white cabinets on every wall and a dining room next to it, where Mom had her first Duncan Phyfe dining room suite.

We were there come Christmas time because the neighbor made us the gifts that I spoke about, and Wayne got a green Ford car that year for Christmas. It was one of those toys that you would give a few short pushes, and it would take off by itself. Those cars were the rage for little boys at the time, and Bruce Price had a large collection that covered the living room at Christmas. Mother found out that his mother would put up his cars after Christmas and would not let him play with them. The next year she would buy him more cars and drag the older ones out again and put them under the tree. So it appeared that Santa gave him way more than other kids got. Mom was furious with Juanita.

While we were living in Pocomoke, it was the only time I was in the

Brownies at school. We made bird feeders for the birds out of pine cones, peanut butter, and bird seeds and brought them home to hang in the trees when there was snow on the ground. I did not ride the bus but lived so close that I walked to school with someone. I have no clue who that might have been.

I came home from school one day and it must have been Brownie meeting day, as I was in my uniform, and mother had a job for me. Mother found out that a family that lived down the street from us was having a hard time. She handed me a bag, a basket, or maybe a box of food and told me to take it to them. There were steep steps up to the front porch, but I made it and rang the doorbell. A woman answered the door and had her hair all tied up in strips of paper bags. I had never seen that before, and she scared the B-Jesus out of me, so I yelled, and ran all the way home with my load. I remember Mom being upset with me and making me go back down there with her to deliver the care package. Mother was always giving and helping anyone she could.

The woman who lived nextdoor to us in a beautiful old home was named Mrs. Bounds. She had a high white wooden picket fence with a fancy gate and arches. There were flowers growing everywhere in Mrs. Bounds backyard with lots of trees and birds singing. She too had a Victorian kitchen with white cabinets everywhere, but she had a booth in her kitchen, and I loved to sit there. I do not remember anything else about our move to Pocomoke City except that Mother shopped at the A&P on Main Street, and I used to love to go in that store with her just so I could smell the fresh-ground coffee.

I was in the third grade when we moved there, so we must have lived there for at least a-year-and-a-half. It may have been while we were living in Pocomoke that Mom and Dad had the new kitchen, bath and back porch added on. I do remember everybody going back to the house in Marumsco in the evening and my parents scraping off the wallpaper in the living room. They would have to soak it with water many times with some kind of contraption they bought as it was taking too long by hand. There was a bazooka and a machete laying on that floor that they had left there when we moved. Both of them came from Briddells in Crisfield where Mom and Dad worked during WWII. We kept going there every evening so they could paint, paper, and work on the house. One night when we got there someone had busted in the door and stolen the war weapons.

I know we moved back to Marumsco at the end of my fourth grade because my teacher, Reba Long, put me in the school band with another girl named Lois Long, and we were the majorettes. Someone made us white satin outfits with hats, and the highlight of my career was marching in the parade at the Crab Derby in Crisfield with the bigger bands. Whoever our bandleader was kept telling us the most important thing to *not* do that day was to not drop the baton in front of the judges' stand. Ironically, I found a picture of the two of us in one of Mary Jo's yearbooks and made a copy. It appears there was no money for white boots, since she and I both are wearing black shoes in the picture.

With the recent death of Queen Elizabeth, I realized that the addition was built while we were living in Pocomoke City, which explains why I do not remember carpenters being at our house. During the Queen's funeral, I had a flashback of seeing her on the day she was crowned, and I clearly remember where the TV was when I watched her coronation seventy years ago.

Wayne Matthews (l)
and Allen Matthews (r)

Joyce Matthews
9 months

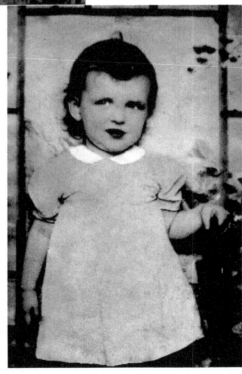

THE DEVIL CAME TO LIVE WITH US

Mother's oldest sister, Mary Collett, had a rough life trying to support herself and six children. She had three daughters and three sons, and the kids would visit with Mom and Dad, Uncle William and Aunt Thalia, and Aunt Willie Mae in the summertime. I barely remember the summer that the two oldest girls, Charlotte and Mary Louise, came to visit, but I do remember their sister, Betty Ann, who spent the summer with us. I remember because she is the one who went out in that shed in the backyard and turned it into a playhouse for me. There were a bunch of window screens out there and she used them for room dividers and gathered wooden boxes to make furniture that she draped with some type of fabric. It was a great playhouse and the only one that I ever had. I was out there with the water hose one day spraying off the cobwebs that hung from the rafters. All of a sudden, I was spraying a huge old black snake and he fell to the floor. I screamed and ran to the back door in such a hysterical panic, I could not even tell anyone what had happened. Mother was there and so was John Barber, who was trying to make sense of whatever I was screaming.

Their brothers, Charles and Robert Barber, came also, but I do not remember much about them, except that Robert and I hung out a lot together when he was there. Then there was the brother, John Barber, the oldest boy who came and stayed—the devil in sheep's clothing. He would come for a while, then leave and go home. I think he kept getting in trouble and would come back again. I do not know how old I was when he climbed up on the roof of that single-story addition at Christmastime and pretended to be Santa Claus and scared the heck out of Wayne and me. It was Christmas Eve, and I guess we were told many times to go to bed but we didn't listen. I know we got in that bed when we heard that noise on the rooftop.

So, I was still young enough to believe in Santa, and Wayne and I slept in the same bed. Phyllis might have been in the room with us also. John Barber must have been sleeping on the daybed as there were only two bedrooms upstairs. He started coming into our room and crawling in the bed between Wayne and me or Phyllis and me. I would be awakened with his hand over my mouth as he whispered in my ear telling me to keep quiet. I know there were two double beds in that room. Soon he started molesting me every night, and I have no clue how long this went on. It could have been weeks, months, or years for all I know. I was so young and afraid that I was going to have a baby, not knowing what all was involved. I was terrified and knew that Daddy would beat me with his belt if he knew what was going on, so I kept it a secret. What stands out the most is me telling John Barber that I was tired and just wanted to sleep. I even cried at times because I wanted to sleep after I had played hard all day. I know now what he was trying to do and thank God it never got to that point. I was always happy when he left to go back home and scared to death when he would come back.

There was a little girl who used to ride our bus to school and she lived near the old wooden bridge that crossed Marumsco Creek. She had long brown hair that she wore in pigtails, and she had lots of freckles. I remember how dirty her face looked at times and she always looked like she had been crying when she got on the bus. One day some people who were all dressed up came to our elementary school and took the little girl. I remember hearing that the little girl was being molested by a family member every night and that she had gone to live in a foster home. I am not certain that the threat of being taken away to a foster home didn't play a part in my decision to keep the ordeal at our house a secret.

When I got a little older, John left me alone, but I did not trust him. He returned when I was a teenager and I was getting out with friends on occasion. At this time, I had my own bedroom, and I do not know where he slept. Hopefully, it was not in the bedroom with my younger siblings. He got a job at Mrs. Paul's Kitchen in Crisfield where Mother and Berky worked. It was there that he met a girlfriend named Ruth and they eventually married. They moved to Deep Creek and maybe had a child. Mother kept up with them and told me that Ruth had a lot of mental issues.

I did not tell anyone what had happened with the exception of one person who died many years ago. As the years passed, I would bury it deep into the back of my brain. Then I would hear on the news about a child being molested by a family member, and I would dwell on it again. I had a friend, Debra, who used to visit me here in Deltaville and she had been molested by her uncle. She would come here and talk to me about it, as she was in counseling at the time, but still I kept quiet. I learned through census research that John Barber was seven years older than I was.

Mother would call me and tell me that Aunt Mary Collett and some of the family was coming to visit and that they would like to see me. I always made an excuse why I could not come from Maryland to spend time with them. Once, I was at my parents' house in Syringa and we were getting ready to eat dinner. It was in the summer and the weather was nice. Here came this huge black tractor trailer up the lane. Everyone was puzzled as to what it was doing there, and you guessed it. John Barber climbed down from that rig and walked in the house. It was the first time I had seen him in years. I went outside, got in my car, and drove somewhere until he was gone.

It was sometime in the '90s when I decided if we were to lose mother, I would forbid him from coming on the property. As fate would have it, John Barber died in 1999 from lung cancer. Sometime around 2002 or 2003, I was visiting my mother, and we were talking about a dozen or more things when I told her about John Barber, and asked why she didn't put a stop to it. I got upset and cried, then she got upset and cried, but she said she never knew about it. I have convinced myself since then that she was probably working the night shift in a nursing home and was never there when it occurred.

Daddy used to go to Lawrence Burgess' store to play cards when Mom was working, so for all I know, neither of my parents was in the house when it occurred. Now I am reminded of those nights when I hear stories about family members molesting children, and I want to scream. Had he been living when mother passed away, I would have done everything within my power to put him in prison for years. One thing is very clear: I am not as Christian and forgiving as my grandmother Amy or Aunt Josie were because I hope John Barber is rotting in hell to this day.

I was very aware of who was around my children like a mother cougar when they were young, probably more than any sane person would admit. I walked down the hallway one day when we lived on Feathered Head in Columbia, Maryland to see my ex sitting on the side of Terrie's bed watching her sleep. John Wayne had a line in an old movie, something to the effect of man has seen no hell, until he has seen the wrath of a scorned woman. You can take one that to the bank.

Our Trips out of Somerset

When I was very young—I may have been the only child at the time—we would go to Baltimore City to visit with my parents' friends, Mary Lee Sawyer and her husband Eddie Waters. It was there that I would see this Black man driving a wagon with a pony, and the wagon was loaded with fruits and vegetables. He would drive the streets yelling whatever he yelled, and everyone would go out and buy from him. On the front of the wagon there were poles with bunches of bananas hanging from them, and Daddy would always go out and buy me a banana. Whenever we were there, Mother and her friend would take the trolley car and go downtown to the stores, so Mother took me on the trolley car with her. The tracks were everywhere. It would be many years after those rides before I would ride another trolley car—not until I went to San Francisco in my twenties.

On one of those trips to Baltimore they took the Waters' son, Eddie, and me downtown at nighttime. We got to see all the Christmas displays set up in the store windows, and there were dolls and toys in every window. I was in awe when I saw the mannequins that looked like real people dressed in fancy winter clothes standing in winter scenes. The one I remember the most was a huge window set up with trains going in every direction. I had never seen an electric train before, and it was not something that I forgot.

When I was little, Mary Price's sister, Virginia Ward from Deltaville, would come to visit Mary. One of their relatives owned a huge old hotel on the boardwalk in Ocean City. Mrs. Ward would pick me up and take me to Ocean City for the week. There was a huge porch loaded with big white Adirondack chairs across the front of the hotel and sand between the porch and the boardwalk running parallel to the ocean. There were other kids there to play with, and it was a great week. I recall lots of bedrooms in the house, but we all had to share a bathroom at the end of the hall. We ate our meals in a huge dining room that overlooked the ocean.

We did get a family vacation away from home in the summertime when Mother always went to North Carolina to spend one or two weeks with her family. I guess Daddy did not get vacations wherever he was working, as he always took us there, dropped us off, and came back sometime later to get us. I would cry when Daddy left us and wanted him to stay there too.

I was always in awe of the beautiful blooming Crepe Myrtles between the highways in Virginia and North Carolina and intrigued by the huge tractor trailers. One trip sticks out in my mind. I think it was a Fourth-of-July trip. It was hot and late in the day, and when we got close to the ferry, the traffic was backed up for miles. I remember all of us kids piled in the back of the car just sitting there sweating and not moving in that traffic. Mother spotted a farmhouse that was probably 200 or 300 hundred feet off the road. There were a couple of green glass soda bottles in the floorboard, and she grabbed them and walked to that farmhouse to get water for us kids. Daddy crept along as traffic moved a little, and I was panicking that she was going to get left behind. He didn't leave, though, and she came back with bottles of water, fussing that the pump was on the screened porch and the woman would not even pump it a few times to cool off the water but gave Mom bottles of hot water. I can still hear her fussing about it, but I guess we drank the hot water.

I loved the ferry rides across the bay, and saw many things I had never seen before. In fact, we watched the progress from year-to-year as they built the Chesapeake Bay Bridge Tunnel. Daddy would walk us around from one deck to the other so we could see the sights. One day, we were walking past the dining room and they must have been serving breakfast or brunch. I spotted a waiter with plates of waffles loaded with whipped cream and strawberries. That was the prettiest dessert I had ever seen, and I wanted it. I did not get it, and I do not recall us ever getting anything to eat from that restaurant. No doubt, Mother took our food in the car for us to snack on as there was no money for such luxuries.

On another trip, I was sitting in the ferry's lounge with my mother, and there was a woman with a little girl sitting across from us. The other girl and I were exchanging looks and smiles, and she started playing with this doll with long pigtails. She opened a funny-looking box that was loaded with clothes, shoes, and other items for her doll baby. It was a doll suitcase, and I had never seen one before. I just drooled with envy. I did not know that doll babies had all those different clothes because mine didn't. I never got a suitcase for my dolls either.

One of my more shocking memories on another trip happened in that lobby when a huge Black woman came and sat across from Mom and me. She had a crying baby in her arms. She started to get undressed, I thought, as she unbuttoned her dress, shirt, or whatever she was wearing and flung out this big thing. I was dumbfounded. That baby latched onto it and quit screaming. Mom kept trying to divert my attention, but I had never seen anything like that before and wanted to watch.

My love for the ferries vanished some years later when Aunt Willie Mae, Aunt Thalia, Uncle William, and I do not know who else, came to the Eastern Shore to visit us. Aunt Willie Mae was still hysterical when she got to our house, as something had gone wrong with their ferry trip. They were the last car to board and somewhere communications went bad. When the ferry pulled off from the dock, the car behind them went overboard and she had seen it go in the water. I do not know the details, but I know that, when it was time to go back home, they had to drive north and west to get back home, as she was never riding that ferry again.

The biggest tragedy I remember when we were traveling was when Aunt Willie Mae had bought me a green balloon on a stick, and gave it to me right before we left to go back home. I was in the backseat with the window down, and somehow my balloon got away from me and blew out the window. We were on a divided highway in North Carolina, and I watched in horror as my balloon blew into the median strip where those beautiful pink Crepe Myrtles grew. Daddy pulled over to get the balloon, and it blew to the other highway. All of a sudden, a tractor trailer hit the brakes and stopped on the stick that was attached to my balloon. I remember that truck driver bringing the balloon to me in the car. Can you imagine a tractor trailer driver stopping on the highway today to save a balloon?

I do remember Daddy getting stopped by the police one day for speeding when I was in the car with him. I cried so hard and pleaded with him not to put my Daddy in jail. He let my father go without a ticket.

Uncle William ran a service station in South Mills, and Mom and Dad always stopped there on the way home once they had left Grandaddy Alex Jones' house. Phyllis remembers that Uncle William would give us kids ice cream at that station.

The events I remember while we were visiting North Carolina are written in the narrative about my mother.

Looking back, it appears that we were blessed with more than one or two grandparents. There were many adults who mentored us in so many different ways and took us under their wings. Such is the story of Aunt Agnes Hoffman, Mom-Mom Amy's sister whom she lived with. Aunt Agnes was the Avon lady in Crisfield and went everywhere in a taxi cab. She sold Avon to everybody in Crisfield, and she would take me to the crab-picking houses whenever she went to Jersey Island, as it was called. There was a creaky old wooden bridge that you had to cross to get there, and the island was built on oyster shells everywhere. The place did not smell good at all because of the the crab houses. They were filled with Black women who would sing and pick crabs all day long, dressed in white uniforms with hair nets on. Aunt Agnes would go there during their lunch time and sell them her Avon products. Then she would go back on Fridays when they got paid to collect her money. She pulled this little cart on wheels loaded with powders, perfumes, and other cosmetics and made a living doing this for years.

Aunt Agnes took me to the Baptist Temple to see the women's choir sing. They were female Masons, I think, and they were known as The Eastern Star. All the women on stage wore long white formal gowns and long white gloves with bright blue banners over their shoulders. It was quite a show! Then on one of her trips to Johns Hopkins Hospital in Baltimore, she dragged me along in the taxi cab with her. It must have been a long day because the only thing I remember was her stopping in the rooms to chat with a few patients she knew. We walked long halls and there was this person who had a large tumor on one side of her face. It was the first time I had ever seen a tumor, and she kept telling me how sick that person was and that she needed lots of prayers.

Aunt Agnes took me to Memorial Day services at the cemetery in

Crisfield. American flags would be draped everywhere, and I had no clue what it meant. There were speakers on the stage and folding chairs for everyone to sit in. It was only when I was older that I learned her husband, Carl Hoffman, was a WWI veteran, and he is buried there on that corner of Chesapeake Avenue in Crisfield. It is in the same cemetery that she and Mom-Mom Amy and their brother, Wells Marshall, are buried. Aunt Agnes had a lady-friend who lived in one of the big old Victorian houses near the cemetery, and we would go there and sit on her front porch. The woman would always go inside and get the candy dish with the same Brach's white candy with some kind of jelly in it, and I did not like it. I don't know who she was, but Mother used to visit her also. Possibly she was a member of the Marshall family.

Grover A. Matthews holding his son Lake
S. Matthews (my father) - taken in Marion
Station, MD in the Spring of 1917.
Lake was born October 5, 1916.

MARION HIGH SCHOOL

Marion High School was Dad's Alma Mater, graduating in 1935. It is where I went to school until I quit at the beginning of my eleventh year. It is where Wayne and Phyllis went to school until they moved to Virginia in 1960.

During my tenure, it was air raid drills that took center stage. All the way through school, everyone expected Russia to bomb the United Sates at any time. The air sirens would go off, and we would all have to get as far under our desks as we could and put our hands over our heads. Later on, they decided we should go into the long hallways farther away from the classroom windows, kneel on the floor, and put our arms over our heads. If we were outside on the school grounds for recess when the alarm went off, we all got into a ditch that surrounded the property and again covered our heads. I remember seeing the big yellow signs on buildings when we went to town showing where the bomb shelters were located. I recall the notices on TV of how much food and water to have in your storm cellar (bomb shelter) in case we were bombed. Hiding in a storm shelter in that low-lying county you would probably have drowned.

Don't ever think the talk of bombs did not scare little children. It became a never-ending dream of mine. Khrushchev was in power at the time in Russia, and that is what the adults talked about. I kept dreaming that he was flying over our house and had three bombs hanging from ropes on that plane. I was terrified that one of those bombs was going to hit our roof. I woke up more than once crying or panicked from that dream. At some point, I even drew a picture of what I had envisioned in my mind.

Not only could you count on air raid drills every year, but also May

Day festivals in which every child in every grade participated. In the first or second grade, I recall the mothers getting creative with rolls of crepe paper to make all the kids in the class outfits of fairytale characters. All the little girls dressed like Little Bo Peep, Mary had a Little Lamb, etc. The crepe-paper pantaloons and dresses were very cute, and there was a crook made for Mary that owned the lamb.

May Day included clowns, the elementary school band, and a May pole dance in which the older kids participated. There was a May Queen, and the girls in high school would go around the community collecting fresh flowers to decorate the queen's throne and that of her court. Mother would take me shopping for a new dress for the event. One year, I found a white dress with green stripes at a dress shop in Crisfield, as I was in the May pole dance. I remember the dress was expensive, and I knew that we could not afford it, but Mother put it on layaway until she could buy it.

I clearly remember my first day of school. I may have been doing fine until Daddy came to check on me at lunchtime. I remember crying and telling him I wanted to go home. He told me I had to stay there and that he would see me when I got home. To console me, he went to the cafeteria and bought me an ice cream. It was a Darlene Bar, and it was probably the first time I had ever had one.

Other than that, my memories surround learning to read from our *Dick, Jane and Sally* books. Their orange tabby cat's name was Puff, and their dog's name was Spot. "See Spot run, see Spot jump..." I don't remember what the heck Puff did.

My teacher's name was Mrs. Chamberlain and her daughter, Ann, was in first grade also. One day Ann, a bunch of other girls and I were outside playing at recess, and there was a huge waterhole. We decided to see who could jump across the waterhole, and every one of us got our shoes and socks soaked. When the bell rang, and we came inside, Mrs. Chamberlain sent all of us to the office except her daughter Ann. That was my first lesson about how it is not what you know but who you know. Myrtle Todd was our principal and her office was upstairs. She had a big wooden paddle on her desk and it scared the B-Jesus out of us. I do not remember what our punishment was, but we did not get hit with that paddle. That was the one and only time I ever got sent to the principal's office.

In the second grade, like a few others, I had a teacher who had taught Daddy when he attended school there. Her name was Elizabeth Cullen. She was an older woman who wore her hair in a bun, longer dresses than most wore at the time, and the typical black laced-up shoes with a low heel. She had a pleasant smile, but was hell on anyone who acted up in her class. She was old-school no doubt, as she still had a tall wooden stool and a dunce's hat that stood in the corner of the classroom. If that was not enough to put the fear of God in any child, she also possessed a thick wooden paddle with a long handle and a hole drilled in the opposite end. There was a boy in my class named Harry Reams, and Harry and Mrs. Cullen had this thing going. Every day she would call Harry to her desk and instruct him to put his hands on the desk, and every day she would crack him across the knuckles with that paddle. I guess it depended on what he had done as to how many times she hit his knuckles. Then he would have to sit on the stool in the corner wearing the dunce's hat. Numerous boys got cracked that year with the paddle, but Harry's name and butt were plastered to the stool. I do not remember what Mrs. Cullen taught us, except to keep your head low, keep your mouth shut, and keep reading.

In the third grade, I had a young teacher named Mrs. Keenan, and she was pretty but had been born with only one finger on one of her hands. That did not stop her a bit and she wrapped that one finger around a piece of chalk, a pencil or pen, and kept on getting it. I liked her a lot but was in her class only a few weeks when we moved to Pocomoke City. So, I started the fourth grade in Pocomoke City. It's strange that I have no clue what the teachers' names were in Pocomoke City. Maybe I was only there in body and not in soul.

We moved back to Marumsco before my fourth-grade class ended and I was in Reba Long's class. Mrs. Long's classroom was on the end of the building, where there was nothing but windows at the back of the classroom. In every windowsill, Mrs. Long had fancy ceramic flower pots painted with different jungle animals. She had plants growing in each of them and would let the kids take turns watering the plants. She is the teacher who put me in the elementary school band. I recall one day we were doing something, maybe show-and-tell in front of the class, when all of a sudden there was a great commotion. Mrs. Long was holding her head and making weird noises. There were kids surrounding her after someone had broken off a lead pencil point by hitting her in the back of the head with the pencil. There was blood dripping from the back of her head. I do not know if it was an accident or intentional, but you guessed it. It was that rascal Harry Reams acting up again. One has to wonder what ever happened to Harry.

Fifth grade was terrific and our teacher, Leana Revell, was one sweet lady. She was the one who had given Mother the little collie puppy for me when Pal got killed in the muskrat trap. I saw her in Daddy's school picture when he was in the first grade, and she looks much older than him. I continued to stay in the band as a majorette, and that year we got to march in the crab derby parade in Crisfield. I found a picture of Lois Long and me in an old yearbook. I joined the 4-H club when I was in her class, not to cook but to learn to sew. Mrs. Hattie Swift, who used to sew Phyllis' and my clothes, helped me a lot, teaching me how to piece patterns together and put in zippers. By the time I was in the sixth or or seventh grade, I made a pretty pink sleeveless dress with a full skirt and a zipper up the back for a 4-H project.

Before I knew it, I was in the sixth grade, and somewhere along the way, I got really good at spelling. I entered all the spelling bees and stayed near the top. It was a challenge that I liked. Daddy was the one who pushed me with his books and knowledge. In fact, I still have his *Old World Atlas* from which he was always teaching me where the different states were and the names of the state capitals. It was his darn math problems that, I am convinced to this day, were trick questions. If two ducks were in front of two ducks and two ducks behind two ducks and two ducks between two ducks, how many ducks were swimming in the pond? Then there was the one about the train. If an eastbound train was doing eighty miles per hour and there were 3200 miles of track, how long would it take for a west bound train to get to California, or something dumb like that.

Dad had a love for poetry and history, and he had two black-and-white tablets that he had saved from his high school days loaded with poems from Longfellow and Whittier. They had two clubs in school and you either belonged to one or the other and I believe he was in the Whittier club. He also was a fan of Rudyard Kipling's poems and would recite them. But his favorite poem was titled "Trees" written by a man named Joyce Kilmer. Yes, I believe that is where my name came from. Daddy taught me that poem word for word when I was a young child. I do not remember all of it today but have it in print.

Trees

I think that I shall never see,
A poem as lovely as a tree.
A tree whose hungry mouth is pressed
Against the earth's sweet flowing breast.
A tree that looks at God all day,
And lifts her leafy arms to pray.
A tree that might it summer wear
A nest of robins in her hair.
Upon whose bosom snow has lain,
Poems are made by fools like me,
But only God can make a tree.

I found a copy of the poem a few years ago and placed it in the front of Dad's *Old World Atlas* with a note for my kids to find one day.

The day that Dad passed away, I lived in Maryland and did not get home until that night. When I arrived, Phyllis told me they had been to the funeral home and picked out a casket and that I could go to pick out a gravesite. I went with Mother to Windsor Gardens the next day, and she asked me to select a burial plot while she completed the paperwork. They had just planted a row of young oak trees around the circle at Windsor Gardens, and I remembered Daddy's love of the poem, "Trees." I chose a spot in front of one of the young oaks, and today it is a large oak that gives shade over their graves.

Things started getting tough in that sixth year of school, as our teacher, Ms. Carrie Gumby, had taught Dad when he was in elementary school. She was a tall woman who wore her hair in a bun and long dark dresses and never smiled, but she yelled a lot. If there ever was a general in Marion High School, it was Ms. Gumby. Every subject was getting harder and she was all-hands-on-deck. In hindsight, we probably learned more in her class than any other. She was prepping us to take that next big step to seventh grade. We stepped up in more than one way, as we now got to move upstairs. Grades One through Six were held downstairs and Six through twelve were housed upstairs.

One of the saddest events of my childhood happened when I was in the sixth grade. We went to school with a lot of Mennonite children and one of the boys in my class was Calvin Kurtz. Calvin had a brother in the grade above us and two more brothers in high school. His family owned a large dairy farm in Rehobeth, and he spoke often in front of the class about having to get up at 5:00 am for them to get all the cows fed and chores completed before getting on the school bus. Everyone loved the Kurtz kids and respected them. Calvin's mother gave birth to a baby, but both she and the baby died during childbirth.

The funeral was in the little wooden church where the Mennonites worshiped, and they took all the kids from the boys' classes to the funeral. We all stood in the back of the church and each was given a flower. One-by-one, we marched to the front of the chapel, and there was Mrs. Kurtz lying in an open casket with her baby in her arms. The baby was dressed in a white crocheted hat with a matching shawl wrapped around it and it appeared that Mrs. Kurtz was looking at the baby. We laid our flowers on top of the casket and marched on. I have no clue who came up with the idea, but it was a horrible vision to instill in young children's minds. I could not get the image out of my head for years to come and have only seen one other deceased child since. I can still see both of those children clearly as I write this. The other child was a three-year-old who fell out of a window onto the cement sidewalk in Baltimore City. His young parents brought him back to Crisfield to be buried, as that is where they were were from. A dead child is not something anyone wants to see.

The second thing that happened that year was Hurricane Hazel taking out Pop-Pop Grover and his family's homeplace, which I describe in a different chapter. Yes, it seemed like the world was beginning to turn faster than I could keep up.

I bought lunch sometimes at school and took it other times. The only thing that I remember being on their menu that I liked was corned beef hash and applesauce which were served with green beans. I loved the corned beef hash and hated the green beans. I still do. Whenever I took my lunch, it was always a potted meat sandwich in a paper bag. I liked it, but not until it got warm and mushy, so I would keep half of the sandwich and eat it on the school bus heading home when it was warm and mushy.

Like all kids, I started seventh grade with great expectations and excitement. That was, until I came home with my first report card, and the first grade on it was a big "F." Algebra got me and got me good. Daddy had been the one engaged in our school work and the response that he came up with was, "The only thing I ever learned in algebra was that x equals the unknown, and I still do not know what the unknown was." My best friend, Sue Ann Menzel, had also gotten an F, so she and I decided we would challenge each other to see who could get the best grade next time. We both pulled our grade up to A.

We had maybe two older teachers in high school, Mrs. Morgan and Mrs. Landon, but otherwise they were young teachers. I liked most of them with the exception of Mr. Caitlin's science class where he insisted the girls partake in the dissection of birds, frogs, etc. I could not stand that bloody mess, but I loved Mrs. Taylor and her husband, Raymond. They both were in sports along with other subjects, and I loved being in Mrs. Taylor's art class. It was she who taught me how to draw people and animals, and she would put me on school projects drawing classroom murals and using chalk for paint. It was Raymond Taylor who threw a softball when I was not looking and broke my nose. I was the catcher that day, and by the time I got home, I could not see out of my eyes for the swollen nose. I can still feel the pain.

There was another advantage of moving into the seventh grade and that was our lunch hour. After lunch, the kids were allowed to turn on the record player in the gym and dance the remainder of the hour away. This was the scene of the older students in the school and mostly the girls, except on rainy days. Before we knew it, those juniors and seniors were grabbing us younger girls by the hands and teaching us how to jitterbug. The music was loud, and the words were jumbled, and it was fantastic with Jerry Lee Lewis singing "Great Balls of Fire," and Elvis Presley singing "Blue Suede Shoes." The girls danced their hearts out dressed in those full skirts with all the starched crinolines and Oxford saddle shoes.

Poodle skirts were all the rage at some point, but I did not have one for a long time. Mother always worked hard to get me new things when she could, and she came through with a beautiful poodle skirt at Christmas time. I remember it was brown with a huge white poodle on it that had a puffy pink nose, and a pink collar and leash that wrapped around the front of the skirt. Santa also brought a pink cardigan to match the dog accessories with a little white fur collar on it. I remember trying to collect as many crinolines as I could, and when I washed them, I would use all of Mom's Kings Starch to make them stiff and hang them on the clothesline to dry. It got to the point that she fussed because I used so much of her starch and one of the girls at school told me to use sugar water to stiffen them, so I did. From then on, when I would hang them on the clothesline, they would get stiff as a board. I was in heaven with my brown-and-white Oxford saddles, my crinolines, and poodle skirts. That was all that any teenage girl could ever wish for.

Another must-have, was a collection of little silky scarves that you tied around your neck, and the more colors you had the better you looked. I remember starting out with a red, a black, and a white one. Every time I went to school, someone would show up with another color, and the rest of us would drool. We would turn our button-up cardigan sweaters around backward and tie the scarves on our necks. There was an older girl who lived in Rehobeth by the name of Jean Bell, and her clothes were passed down to me—which I proudly wore. It never crossed my mind that my classmates had probably seen her already wear the pretty outfits.

I suppose most of us had the small record players that looked like a suitcase and played 45 records. Record players and train cases were must-haves for the girls. A train case was a small box-like suitcase that would hold everything you needed for a sleepover at a friend's house.

All the boys were into Ivy League shirts and pants and duck haircuts. They wore white socks and white t-shirts in the summertime, and we jitterbugged and jitterbugged some more. Some of the kids would have parties at their houses on Friday nights, and the times Daddy would let me go (which wasn't often), we would all take our collections of 45s, roll the rugs back on the living room floor, and dance. But those parties interfered with Daddy's nights to play cards with his friends. I remember being promised all week that I could go, then he would upset the apple cart that evening. Mother would be working, and he would take off and leave me there with my younger siblings.

I got my first job around that time, and I loved it. In the front yard of one of the old Victorian homes in Marion Station, the owners put a small trailer out near the road. They sold hot dogs, chips, drinks and maybe candy. I got the job there at the take-out counter and they may have paid me seventy-five cents per shift. I only worked a couple hours in the evenings and a few hours on Saturday. I believe the couple that owned it were friends with my parents.

My best friend, Sue Ann Menzel, had an older sister, Helen Jane. My mother and their mother, Hazel, worked at Mrs. Paul's Kitchen in Crisfield together on the night shift. When Helen Jane got her first car, a used 1949 Ford, she would take Sue Ann and me to the movies or to school events with her. They would come to pick me up on a Friday night, and I would have to tell them I could not go because Daddy was not home.

The Menzels lived in Shelltown down on the Pocomoke River, which was below Rehobeth Baptist Church. I used to go to the Menzels and spend the night on weekends when Mother was not working. Sue Ann, Helen Jane, and I decided to go down to the river to mess around in the water. When we got there, Helen Jane suggested we jump in the river from the dock, and I just stood back and watched as I was not jumping off any dock in dark water. She made fun of us and called us sissies, took off running on the dock, and took a big dive. When she came up, she had this long green thing around her neck and went into a screaming panic. We all screamed, and she was in the water with this thing still around her neck and they both were flopping around. It turned out to be an eel, and she finally managed to free herself from it. It was probably stunned from her screaming so loud. I believe she was a junior in high school at that time. Another day that summer she was sunbathing in her front yard, lying on her stomach. She felt something touch her leg and thought it was a bug, so she kept shaking her leg trying to get the bug or grasshopper off. She finally leaned up to look, only to see a large snake sunbathing across her leg. There was one little country general store across the road, and she ran there for help. She told the stories everywhere we went from then on.

I sat on those old wooden steps in front of the house many Friday nights listening to the frogs croaking and cried. One night I was sitting out there crying because my ride to the movies had just left and Daddy had told me I could not go. He went out the back door and shot his gun up in the air to scare me back into the house. As much as I loved him, he was a chip off the old block, his father Grover. All teenagers go through turbulent times with their parents. Was mine any different? Probably not, but it sure seemed so at that time.

We did our teenage pranks here and there also. Helen Jane and Sue Ann came to pick me up one evening to go somewhere, and before we went home, we decided to go to Vessey's Orchard and grab some apples. Helen Jane stopped the car (her '49 Ford), and Sue Ann and I went into the orchard to get a few apples, which we put in the tails of our shirts. While we were in the orchard, Helen Jane saw car lights headed up the road, and fearing it was the police, she left the area. When we came out of the orchard, she was not there and we were stranded in the dark countryside with shirttails full of apples. There was a big screaming match between the sisters when she finally came back to get us, and we never did that again.

One of the most daring events—and the worst trouble I ever got into—was on a Sunday evening. That Sunday after church I was at another friend's house by the name of Helen Bell. She lived on the other side of Rehobeth, and we could not wait to go crabbing. We must have been on the road near the water when this car came along with several boys from Crisfield in it who asked if we wanted to ride to Ocean City with them. I recall one was a kid named Jack Swift, one was named David Dorman, and I do not remember who the third one was, but we went with them, and they promised us that we would be back in time for us to get to church in the evening.

How could little country girls be so gullible? Somewhere along the way, they stopped and bought a six-pack of beer in glass bottles, and we were walking in the sand on the ocean. We begged those Crisfield boys to take us back before we got in trouble, but they would just laugh. They decided to go for a swim and it was dark by this time. They handed me the six-pack, which may have been down to three beers by then. I tasted one and spit it out. I still have never drunk a beer to this day because of the way it tasted. I was standing there holding their beer as they swam, and all of a sudden there was a spotlight skimming the water. I guess I knew it was the police, so I tossed the rest of the beer in the ocean, which turned into a shouting match when they discovered their beer had sunk in the Atlantic Ocean.

They finally brought us back, and by this time, it was about 11:00 pm. I don't know who took me to my house, maybe Helen's father, but because we had disappeared that afternoon, our parents had called the local sheriff's department. They, in turn notified the State Police who had teams out searching for us. When I walked in the door, Daddy grabbed his leather belt and beat me with everything he had in him. Then, suddenly, he quit beating me and started crying out loud and telling me how upset he and Mother were as they thought we had been kidnapped or that we had fallen overboard and drowned in the creek. It was obvious they were shaken badly, as any parent would be. It was clear he did not believe me when I told him what had happened, and I doubt that I was allowed to go there again. I was maybe thirteen years old at the time, and that was the one and only time he ever hit me with that leather belt, so compared to him, I suppose I was the lucky one.

We had what was called a declamation speech contest every year in high school. We would have to pick out a story that we were interested in learning and then get in front of the class and recite the story, throwing everything we had into the presentation. In the ninth grade I ordered a declamation titled "White Lilacs," and it was about a deaf woman. I was one of the winners from the ninth grade (they always chose two) and then we would go to Princess Anne or Salisbury to compete. Don't you know that I contracted measles and could not go to the competition? My heart was broken. I did tell the story on Mother's Day at Rehobeth Baptist Church. Recently, I stumbled across the old declamation and put it in a folder. One day my kids will find it and wonder what it is.

Like all schools, we had our yearly field trips, and most were to sights or parks in the local areas. Then in the tenth grade, we went to Washington D.C. and what a trip it was! We got to go to the capital and watch congress in session. After that, we went to the Smithsonian and saw things that we never knew existed. Our last stop for the day was the National Zoo, and that was the icing on the cake of a perfect day.

One year, maybe in the ninth grade, the high school kids were invited to a radio station in Salisbury. Every Saturday afternoon, they would broadcast kids dancing, just like the *Dick Clark Show* on TV. The kids that liked to jitterbug got to dance on live local TV for an hour and I was included. We were thrilled and proud to have that opportunity.

My outings with friends would continue on weekends when Mother was off from work. Helen Jane Menzel continued to take Sue Ann and me to the movies or to school events with her because my mother and her mother were close friends. It may have been the only way she could get her car at nighttime, and I faintly remember that she had to take her sister with her. On our trips to Crisfield to see a movie, we kept noticing this little place on the corner next to the theatre where kids our age were going and coming through the door. We got brave enough one night to check it out, and it was all over but the shouting match. Painted across the window was the name "Sweet Shop."

When we entered, there were teenagers everywhere. A long soda bar sat at one side and maybe a couple of pool tables in that front section. You walked through double doors and there were booths all around the walls and a juke box on one side. In addition to the main juke box, there were small ones on each table where you could play three songs for a quarter, I believe. The music was loud and the kids were slow dancing and jitter bugging just like Dick Clark's bandstand on TV. The country girls had found a gold mine on the corner of Main Street in Crisfield and we didn't tell our parents. Girls jitterbugged together at that time and the guys were wallflowers. It was a good thing Daddy did not know we were going in the Sweet Shop.

So, every time we got to go to Crisfield, we would leave as early as possible and dance until we would be late to see a movie. It was one night in that sweet shop that I saw a guy standing near the stove on the sideline watching everybody dance. He was wearing gray slacks, and a pink zip-up jacket. Maybe pink was popular for guys back then. He had dark hair and wore it in a drake tail. Every time I looked up, he was looking at me, but I kept on dancing and enjoying the rock 'n roll music with my friends. He stood in front of the juke box, picked some tunes, then walked over and asked me to jitterbug with him. His name was Jerry A. Thomas.

From then on, if we went to Crisfield on the weekends, Jerry would be there and he and I would dance a lot, including slow dances. The Platters and the Everly Brothers were popular artists that were great and we loved to dance to their music, not to mention Jerry Lee Lewis, Elvis Presley and all the Motown artists, but jitterbugging was our thing. We got really good together as time went on. As we headed to the movies one night, Jerry asked if he could join us, and that too became a weekly event if we were there. Jerry loved the Three Stooges and would out laugh anyone in the theatre. There was always a *Three Stooges* episode along with cartoons before the movie started, but we were seldom late as he wanted to see his Stooges.

It was in that movie theatre that I got to see *Jail House Rock* with Elvis Presley, only this time you could see his hip movements. The theatre was jampacked with teenage girls, and they all screamed and jumped up and down like a bunch of jack rabbits. They were so damn loud you could not hear him singing, and I got pissed off at every one of them.

I have no clue how long the fun lasted, as one night when Helen Jane dropped me off, and I walked in the door, my parents were waiting for me with a hundred questions. They wanted to know who was this boy that was seen coming out of the movie with me and walking to Helen Jane's car?

We had a telephone and obviously someone had called them before I got from Crisfield to Marumsco. They asked about the Sweet Shop and had I been there? I had a picture of Jerry hidden in Mom's white wooden cabinet, so I walked over and got the picture and showed it to them and told them what I knew about him. No doubt, the detective, Aunt Agnes Hoffman, went straight to work, and before the week was over, they knew his life history. I was allowed to go to the Sweet Shop and the movies as long as I was with girlfriends, and if Jerry wanted to join us, that was okay if we stayed in the crowd. I learned years later that Aunt Agnes' husband, Carl Hoffman, and Jerry's great-grandmother, Carrie Messick, were siblings, and Mrs. Messick was still living. I have no doubt that is the only reason I was not in deep trouble at the time.

Jerry's parents did not have a telephone, so we could not talk on the phone. Then, all of a sudden, Jerry was nowhere to be found. I guess through Aunt Agnes we learned that Jerry's father, Lewis, had come home on a Friday or Saturday night drunk and gotten into a big brawl with the kids' grandmother, Betty Thomas. Lewis had broken up just about every piece of the furniture in the house, and what he didn't break, he threw out the front door. They were renting an old two-story house that needed painting on one of the side streets behind Bradshaw Funeral Home. I have no idea who showed me where he lived. Jerry had gotten into an altercation with his father trying to protect his mother, and someone had called the cops.

I don't remember when I saw him again or how I learned that Jerry had left the area and joined the US Navy. That news probably came from

Aunt Agnes also, but a good length of time went by before I got a letter in the mail from Jerry. I don't remember what he wrote, but I stuck the letter away somewhere and did not write back to him.

Sometime later, I received another one and Mom had gotten the mail. I read the letter and maybe she did also, but once again I tucked it away. She asked me shortly after that if I had written a letter for her to mail to Jerry. I told her no, and that I didn't want to write to him, that I wanted to do things with my friends and focus on other things and that I did not want a boyfriend. She got angry with me and told me I should have the decency to answer his letter after all he had been through. She said I was not going to run around with kids doing things that were not permissible and that she would put me in a reform school first. She threatened me with that several times when I was a teenager, and I was a good kid. I believe that was a tool that parents used often those days, as my friends talked about the threats also. I sat down and wrote Jerry a letter, and she mailed it.

Betty Thomas called Mom or Dad on our phone and told them that Jerry was graduating from boot camp on such-and-such a day, and that Jerry wanted me to come with his parents and brother to the graduation at Bainbridge Navel Training Station in Maryland. I went with them to the graduation, and wore that turquoise topper that mother had bought me to match hers for Easter Sunday. I recall it was cold and windy that day, and there were a lot of pictures taken but the only one I have is of Jerry, Lewis, and Richard. It was in the pictures that Terrie brought from Maryland.

Jerry was sent to a naval station somewhere in Norfolk or Portsmouth, along with another boy from Pocomoke, I believe. The other guy had a car and would come home on weekends and give Jerry a ride or Jerry would ride home on the Greyhound bus. I don't know when he met my parents, but he started coming to Rehobeth Baptist Church on Sunday mornings in his uniform. He would then go home with us to spend the day, and we would go back to church on Sunday evenings. He would stay at our house until his friend came to pick him up in the evening. John Barber was back living with Mom and Dad at that time. I remember Jerry and I sat in the car one Sunday night waiting for his friend to pick him up and it was cold outside. It got so cold, we had to go in the house, and we were frozen. John Barber jumped all over Jerry because he had kept me outside in the car on a freezing night, and he wanted to know what we had been doing. He was over-protective of me, and it showed.

Jerry and I got married on November 1, 1958 at his parents' home. They had moved to Somerset Avenue in a big old Victorian house right next door to the Church of God that Mom-Mom Amy attended. Mother and Dad were not coming to the wedding, but Mother bought me a pretty little white dress and a white headband that resembled a hat and Jerry wore his Navy uniform. Eleanor Ward (Jerry's aunt) made us a fancy wedding cake with a little bride and groom on top. There was a punch bowl and mints on the table, and I guess it was only Jerry's family there.

Right before the wedding was to begin, someone knocked on the front door, rang the doorbell or something, and it was Dad. He was dressed in his suit and tie and had a camera in his hand, and I was so happy that he was there. He came in and talked with everyone and asked who the preacher was. When he was told it was the preacher that lived next door who was also the preacher for the Church of God, he got upset that it was not a Baptist preacher and walked right out the door with his camera in hand. So, no one took pictures of our wedding that night. So be it....

Steven Dale was born a year later and the day he turned three weeks old, Jerry was deployed to Antarctica for nine months on a navy ship. I got a job working nights in Crisfield and stayed with Jerry's parents. I'm not sure how I got to work, but every once in a while, I stopped in at home. One night I stopped in and there was this older heavy-set Black man sitting with the kids. Mother was working and Daddy was not there. Mom and Dad had opened up the closet under the stairway, and the man was sitting in a blue fake leather chair under the steps. Next to it, Mother had an old buffet that she had painted white and used for storing clothes. The kids were playing on the floor and when Wayne opened one of the doors to the cabinet, a rat came charging out at him. There was a lot of screaming and commotion from everyone, and the old Black man was fighting the rat. It was fighting him back. The rat was showing its teeth, and he killed it right there in the house. No doubt Mother needed me there to help her, but I was no longer there and had already found a job in Crisfield.

Keith Daugherty (6 1/2 months old) and
Margaret Matthews
November 11, 1942
Looks like the old farm to me!

Aunt Agnes has the Last Word

I later rented a small trailer that sat in someone's backyard on Somerset Avenue in Crisfield. It was not far from Jerry's parents and it was close to Mom-Mom Amy and Aunt Agnes' house. I could see their backyard from where Steve and I lived. Steve was a toddler by then, and I would walk with him to see them when the weather was pretty. We would sit on the front screened porch and talk. On this particular day, Mom-Mom Amy was not there, but Aunt Agnes was, which was unusual. We were sitting in what they called their parlor—the sitting room, not the formal front room—and Aunt Agnes had stories to tell. I do not know what the topic was, but she mentioned ten years in the future. I responded that ten years was a long time off, and she told me, "If you think ten years is a long way off, look back on the last ten and see how fast they have gone." It was a statement I have never forgotten. Some years later, I realize how right she was.

Then she got down to nitty-gritty adult conversation, asking if I knew the story about Mom-Mom Amy and Pop-Pop Grover. I didn't know what she was talking about. What I did know was that Mom-Mom Amy was next to the youngest of nine children and Pop-Pop Grover was an only child, a hurdle to overcome from the start. Aunt Agnes proceeded to tell me how badly he had treated her when they were married and that he was a playboy. She said that when the sun went down, he went out in his fancy cars, and in the morning, he would bring his lady friends home. He would frolic with them downstairs as Mom-Mom laid in her bed with Daddy close by and listen to the laughing and whatever else they were doing. Both of his parents were living in the house at that time. She said he eventually moved a mistress in the house who lived there for years. She told of times that she would not hear from Mom-Mom Amy for weeks and would get worried about her. One Sunday night she took a taxi to Rehobeth Baptist Church searching for her. No one had seen her for a long time, and Aunt Agnes told them she only had one dress and described it. At that moment Mom-Mom walked in the church door, and, sure enough, she was wearing that one dress. I would bet she took a horse and buggy or walked to the church services, as no doubt Pop-Pop would not let her drive one of his fancy cars.

Aunt Agnes said that when Mom-Mom finally decided to leave him, Aunt Josie was just an infant. It was during a snowstorm, so he decided to take her to Crisfield in the horse and wagon, and snow was halfway up the wheels of the wagon. Aunt Josie was born on Ground Hog Day, so this had to be in February or March of that year. Aunt Agnes' father, John Marshall, lived at a place called Riggins's Field in Crisfield that was in the boonies. Instead of Pop-Pop taking her and his baby daughter down that road and over a wooden bridge that was on the way to her father's house, he dropped her off at the end of the road and made her walk, toting the infant and whatever luggage she had taken with her in the storm. Mom-Mom Amy came home during this conversation and was in the kitchen but never said a word about it. She had always lived her life as a quiet and mild-tempered angel.

I left there confused and in disbelief. I was well-aware of how grumpy Pop-Pop could be and how he hollered at all of us kids, but I had no idea about the history Aunt Agnes had just shared with me. What does one do with all of this information about your grandfather?

I didn't know what to do, so I kept quiet, but I thought about him in a different way from then on. Whenever I go to Maryland to visit the Matthews graves at Rehobeth Baptist Church, the thought of how he treated Mom-Mom overrides any day-to-day childhood memories I had of him, and we saw him just about every day as we were growing up.

It wasn't until many years later when Mom and Dad were living in Virginia and I was visiting from Maryland, that Dad started talking about family history. He told me about his grandparents and I wrote down everything. I saw it as a perfect time to ask him about what I had heard so long ago from Aunt Agnes. I asked if it was true.

Daddy could be emotional at times, and all of a sudden, he was crying. The tears flowed as he told me about Pop-Pop taking Mom-Mom to Crisfield in the horse and buggy in the blizzard. He said that he made her walk a long distance with his baby sister and luggage through the snow drifts. He said he had never understood why Pop-Pop did that to his mother and that he had lived with the pain for years. Because he was so upset, I did not know how to approach the other part of the story regarding Pop-Pop's escapades with women, so I never did.

One day, I asked Mother if she knew anything about the woman that Pop-Pop supposedly had moved into the house when he and Mom-Mom were married. If I remember correctly, Mom did not recall her name but said that Grover (Pop-Pop) had brought her to Baltimore a couple of times to see Dad. Pop-Pop had gotten sick, and the woman had left him shortly after Mom and Dad married. Mom said that Grover came to Baltimore City and had Daddy take him everywhere in Baltimore looking for her. He was there for weeks searching to no avail. He finally gave up and went back to Somerset County.

Aunt Josie told me that when Grover returned from Baltimore, he went to talk to Cousin Addie who lived on the corner of the Road to Frog Eye. He sent Addie to Crisfield to try to talk Mom-Mom Amy into coming back to live with him. She had moved to Crisfield in 1924, and this was sometime after 1940. I wonder what her response was.

When I started doing the family research after Mother passed away, I went looking for Grover's mistress. I was aware of our grandparents getting married in August, 1910, and the census was taken in April of that year, so I pulled up the 1920 census. There, I found George Matthews, age sixty-nine and wife, Josephine, age fifty-one. Also living in the household was their son Grover, age thirty-one, daughter-in-law Amy, age thirty, and their son, Lake (my father), age three-and-a-half. Also listed was Charlie Smith, Black, age forty-three (raised from a boy) who lived and worked on the farm. George could not read or write, but Josephine could. They owned the farm free of debt.

The 1930 census shows Grover A. Matthews as head of the household. He was listed as forty-one years old and now divorced, having married at age twenty-four, able to read and write and a farmer, not a veteran. His son, Lake S. Matthews, was thirteen at the time and attending school. George A

(Grover's father) age eighty, also not a veteran, had married at age twenty. Josephine (Grover's mother) age sixty-nine, had married at age eighteen. Also listed as living in the house was Alice Culver (white female servant), age thirty and born in Delaware. She was listed as a laborer on the farm. Bingo!

Aunt Josie and I had been communicating back and forth about family genealogy, so I asked her about this and she was well informed on the entire story. She knew about the snowstorm and the horse and buggy incident, and she knew about Alice. She told me that Mom-Mom had returned to the farm in the spring and had actually left Pop-Pop twice. She told Josie that she had no money and that Aunt Josie needed clothes, so she worked in the fields picking strawberries to get money to clothe her. She left the second time on July 5, 1924 and Daddy was crying and begging her not to take his baby sister. He would have been seven years old at the time. Aunt Josie was told that she only had one baby bottle, so Daddy hid her bottle and would not tell anyone where it was that day, causing a big delay in the departure. My guess is that Grover lit one too many firecrackers on his Fourth-of-July celebration.

Aunt Josie said that she and Mom-Mom Amy lived with her grandfather John Marshall at Riggins Field until she was in the fourth or fifth grade. Pop Marshall, as she called him, came down sick, and Mom-Mom could no longer take care of him alone, so they all moved in with Aunt Agnes on Hudson Street. The house that her grandfather rented was loaded with antiques, and Mom-Mom had nowhere to put them, so they walked away and left them there. One item that stuck in Aunt Josie's mind was the old pump organ that sat in the living room.

Aunt Josie said it was hard to get Mom-Mom Amy to talk about the past, but she did ask her why she left her brother on the farm and did not take him with them. Mom-Mom said she did not know how she was going to feed her children, and that Grandmom Jo loved Daddy so dearly, he would be fine there with her. Aunt Josie said that her mother was in court one day for something (maybe divorce proceedings) and the judge suggested she file for child support, but she refused to do it and told the judge she wanted nothing from Grover.

Aunt Josie pulled out some papers to copy and send to me and stumbled on her birth certificate. She called me and said she was shocked. There, in black-and-white, was a witness to her birth, and it was Alice Culver, the mistress. This gave us a timeframe of when she was there. Aunt Josie was born February 2, 1924. So, Alice had moved there sometime after 1920 and was still there in 1940.

Going through my folder of Matthews notes and documents just now, I see the will of Josephine Darby Matthews—Grover's mother who raised my father. It is dated January 19, 1934. It is witnessed by C.F. Matthews and Alice L. Culver.

L to R - Josephine Darby Matthews, Amy M. Matthews with son Lake S.
Matthews others unknown

Aunt Josie Goes to Live on the Farm

Aunt Josie (Dad's sister) started school in Crisfield, and the following summer, the doctor spotted something questionable with her lungs. He suggested it might do her well to go the farm and attend school in the second grade there so she could get lots of fresh air in the countryside. She attended the little school in Marumsco and Dad rode the bus to Marion High School. Aunt Josie got home before him and would change her clothes and rush to the end of the lane to wait for the bus. She said that every day the kids on the bus would laugh out loud at her, but she did not know why. She had no play clothes, so she wore a pair of Dad's overalls when she got home, and they were way too big for her. One day she figured out the kids were laughing at the way she was dressed, so she never went to the end of the lane again, but sat on the hill where the house was and waited for her brother.

She said that even though the meals were cooked in the kitchen on the old woodstove, they always ate in the dining room, as all the dogs lived in the kitchen. One can only imagine how many hunting dogs lived in that kitchen. No wonder they loved biscuits....

Aunt Josie told me they were allowed to pee in the pot, but for everything else, you had to make the trip down the field to the outhouse. One night she got sick in the middle of the night and was scared to go alone, so Alice went to the outhouse with her. When they returned, she asked Alice if she could sleep with her, and she said yes. She said every night for the rest of her visit she slept in the bed with Alice and that Alice was kind to her. She told me that her father would only bring his car out on Sundays, and sometimes they would go to Delaware where Alice's family lived.

Aunt Josie remembered her only Christmas spent there like it was yesterday. Somewhere along the way, she got the idea that she wanted Santa to bring her a goose that laid golden eggs, and she kept telling anybody who would listen. She had no clue where she had seen such a thing, and Santa did not bring one. Instead she got a little tin tea set and two pieces of fabric for Christmas. Both pieces of fabric were identical in a little flowered pattern, but one was blue and the other was pink. Someone made her two dresses, and she rotated wearing them to school.

Aunt Josie said she was out playing on the woodpile one day when she decided she wanted to go back home. She ran and found her father and told him, so he took her home. When they got to the house, he looked at her and said, "You are here, now stay here." She clearly remembered the words. When she was a teenager, she was going to have a birthday celebration and it may have been her sixteenth birthday. She wanted Daddy (her brother) to come, so arrangements were made for him to attend. Pop-Pop brought him in his car, and she went running out to tell her father it was her birthday. Pop-Pop's response was "I know" and he never even wished her a happy birthday. She was crushed.

In addition to his frequent curt comments to her, his only daughter, Josie learned that her father didn't even enter the room after she was born until she was four or five days old. I am sure it was Aunt Agnes who dropped that bomb in her lap. It was something that Aunt Josie never accepted. To make matters worse, when Mom-Mom left him that final time, Aunt Josie was five months old and Pop-Pop still had not held her one time. I am not sure he ever did.

In spite of all that had happened, Aunt Josie would go there every now and then to see family and take her children. She said there was a bench just inside the door and that her three kids would sit there on the bench while she visited. According to her, there was never any interaction between Pop-Pop and his grandchildren. She told me that whenever Steve, her second child, was grumpy, he would make the statement that he must have a touch of Grover in him. If that is the case, I suppose we all do.

The family celebrated Pop-Pop's seventy-fifth birthday at the Matthews farm on August 27, 1963. Mom and Dad were living in Virginia and Aunt Josie and Millard lived in Delaware and everyone went to the celebration. I went and took my three children and we have a few pictures from that day, but not many.

Not long after that, Pop-Pop became sick and ended up in McCready Hospital in Crisfield. Someone was there at the hospital with him most of the time, and he had numerous issues going on. He had surgery to remove varicose veins in both legs and both were bandaged. If I am not mistaken, he died from prostate cancer. I was at the hospital one morning with him when he woke up and asked for a glass of orange juice. I got so excited and couldn't wait to tell Edna. She came to the hospital at noon, and I left after sharing the good news. He passed away early that afternoon on October 15, 1963.

I could not attend his funeral because of my three little ones and no sitter. I was told that Daddy was a total wreck that day and that Aunt Josie never shed the first tear. She brought up the day in one of my conversations with her and said she only wanted to hear one thing that day. So, before they ever entered the church she asked "Bud" (what she called Daddy) if her father had ever made things right with the Lord. Daddy told her that he had. She told me that was the only thing she wanted to hear, and that was good enough for her. She said because it was "Bud" who told her, she believed him.

Our grandfather's legend, in my point of view, is that he was a tall, very handsome man who loved his dogs, his cars, and his women more than his family. I have no clue what order they came in, but we have photos and documentation to back up the stories.

Pop Pop Grover's at his
75th birthday party

Glen Ingram Matthews and Steven Dale Thomas (Glen's nephew)
Taken at Pop Pop Grover's 75th birthday party in Marumsco, MD August 1963

BEHIND CLOSED DOORS

In the '90s, Mary Jo stubbed her toe really bad and could not walk, so she came to stay with me in Maryland for a few months. John and I had just moved into our new house, and he was working in Bermuda most of the time. Mary Jo and I were talking one day about growing up on the shore and of days gone by, when she looked at me and asked if I knew what everyone talked about when Mom and Dad moved to Virginia. Once again, I was clueless. She proceeded to tell me that Mother had an affair and that she had left Dad. Mary Jo said that everyone knew it and it was the talk of the neighborhood. She added that Dad never paid anybody for anything and left there owing a lot of money.

I seem to recall a Bible scripture that went something like "whoever of you is without sin, let him be the first to throw a stone at her." Maybe they were not in church that Sunday and missed the sermon.

Roughly ten years later, when I was visiting Mother, we were talking about the old days on the Eastern Shore. I asked her "whatever happened to him?" She replied that he had gotten married, bought the old house where Reverend Reid and Aunt Annie lived up that lane, remodeled the house, and had died shortly after that. I never mentioned it to her again. According to the census, he married someone named Irma from Baltimore City in 1956 and died in 1965.

Mother had passed away years before when I talked to Aunt Josie about Mom and Dad. She told me that Daddy had brought Mother to Crisfield to meet the family before they got married. Aunt Josie said she was wearing a burgundy wool coat with a big fur collar, and she was "so pretty." We have a picture of Mom in that coat that Aunt Thalia had in her collection and sent to mother in a card right before she passed away. None of us had ever seen the photo before. I asked Aunt Josie about what Mary Jo had told me about Mother leaving Daddy and whether she knew if there was any truth to it. She did know and told me that when Mother left him, he went to Crisfield to Mom-Mom and Aunt Agnes' house. She said he was pitiful and had a mental breakdown, crying all the time.

The only suggestion they could offer was that he should stay home more and quit running back and forth to Baltimore City. I asked Mary Jo if she knew where Mother went, and she said she went to stay with Cousin Annie, our grandfather's cousin. As soon as she said that, I remembered being upstairs at Cousin Annie's when I was very young. I remembered the long banister running along the upstairs hallway that had a lot of dark doors and woodwork and the antique furniture. Then, I asked if she knew why Mom had left him. She answered that there was another party involved and that Daddy had confided in Uncle Millard. She turned around and asked Uncle Millard if he recalled who the guy was that Mother had left Daddy for, and he answered, "That guy who lived around the corner."

Was my father irresponsible or spoiled by his grandparents? Absolutely, but there were countless qualities that would make any child proud of her father. He was the only child and Mother was the youngest of five children. No doubt they had different perspectives and priorities. Although, he went to play cards at Burgess Store, and I wish he hadn't, I do not remember ever seeing him drink a beer or take a drink of liquor. For all we know, he drank root beer while playing cards. He could be grouchy and too strict when I was growing up, but he made it up with his grandchildren, all of them. No one was ever abused or beaten like he threatened with that leather strap— except that one time when my disappearance scared him—even though his father beat him.

After Glen was hurt in the accident and his condition had improved greatly, Dad started taking him out in the car with him often. He soon realized that he could not take him into any of the local businesses in the county because there were no handicap ramps. So, Dad was on a mission. He went to the county and all the local organizations with his concern. I do not know how long it took him, but he accomplished his mission until finally every business in the county had installed ramps or curb cuts so that the handicapped could enter. He was recognized and honored for his efforts by the local organizations and got a great write-up in the local paper.

I don't know how old I was when Dad started going to church in Rehobeth and became very-much involved. My parents had gone to Harmony Grove Baptist Church once they moved to Virginia. Maybe Mother dragged him there. At some point, they moved their memberships to Springhill at Cobbs Creek. It was there that he started teaching Sunday school, and I am told that his name is still on the classroom door. He loved both of his parents and his sister dearly, and when Glen got hurt in 1973, he was there for Glen until the day he died in 1987. When Wayne joined the army, our parents received an 8x10 picture of him in uniform. Dad took that picture of Wayne everywhere he went and showed it to everyone, talking about Wayne with anyone who would listen. He was very emotional about Wayne going overseas since as we were in the middle of the Vietnam war.

As a matter of fact, I only saw our parents get into two arguments during my lifetime, and I was devastated both times. As every community has their town drunk, so did the rural areas. Our local drunk was named Howard Bell, and he used to walk the highway back and forth to Burgess Store all the time. There were a lot of Bells who lived in Rehobeth and they may have been his family. Whoever they were, they kicked Howard out of their house. I faintly remember the conversation with Daddy wanting to bring him to our house and Mother laying down the rules. I have no idea how long he was there, but I remember being upstairs with Mother and she was packing suitcases when it was still daylight. Dad came home and there was a lot of loud talking in the bedroom. That was the only time I ever heard arguing as a child. Mother had found a pint of whiskey somewhere that belonged to Howard Bell, and we were going to North Carolina to live. Wayne may not have been born yet, but I am not certain of that. I cried and cried when she told me we were leaving and Daddy was not going with us. Howard Bell moved out and we didn't, so I can only assume she gave Daddy an ultimatum.

Our parents were always trying to help those in need, I suppose, as they also took in Edna's son, David, when he was a teenager. Pop-Pop Grover had kicked him out of the house. I don't know how long he stayed there, but he did later marry and have three children. Some years later, David would run off the road just below our house, hit a tree, and die in the accident. Mary Jo said they saw the lights from the house and heard the commotion that night but did not know until the next day that it was Edna's son. I did not remember that.

The second argument I witnessed was when Mom and Dad were in The Furniture Barn, a business that Mother started from home after Glen's accident. I didn't realize what it was about, but I was there with them. Mother started to walk out and Daddy threw something, hitting her in the shoulder. That's when all hell broke loose between them. He looked at me and threw forty-plus years of marital bliss in my lap when I heard more that day than I wanted to know. Apparently, at one of Glen's doctors' appointments in Newport News, a receptionist had caught Daddy's attention, and he was going to jump ship, leaving us after all those years. More than likely, he took the entire situation with the receptionist out of context.

I left and went back to Maryland the next day as distraught as one can get. On Monday, emotional and upset, I talked to my lawyer about our parents possibly getting a divorce. My lawyer, Barry Silber, laughed at me when I told him they were my parents and could not do this. He chuckled and told me that every couple that got divorced was usually someone's parents and that it would be okay. He said that my father was having a midlife crisis. In the end, Dad never went anywhere, and I never heard another word about it.

I take that back. There was one other argument, a knockdown one when Daddy blew the roof off the house one night. It was November 1980 and a presidential election year. Daddy was a lifelong Democrat and expected the same from Mother. They went to the polls at two different times that day and Mother voted for that handsome movie actor, Ronald Reagan, instead of the peanut farmer. I believe they referred to them as Reagan Democrats, and that night at the dinner table, the election came up in conversation. All hell broke loose when Mom told Dad she had voted for Reagan, but she held her ground. It's funny now, thinking back on it. He had not told her what to do, and, of course, Reagan won. That had to be an unpleasant place to live for a few weeks or maybe a few years.

Daddy loved his politics, and I joined him numerous times to watch the big events. From the Agnew demise to the inaugurations, we watched together if I was at home. One in particular comes to mind when John F.

Kennedy was sworn into office in 1961. It was a cold snowy day in DC and just as cold and snowy in Syringa, Virginia. We sat in my parents' bedroom, where Dad had put a small stove for heat, and watched on the black & white TV. Some twelve years later, we watched the Watergate hearings against Nixon, and John Dean's testimony got Dad's blood pressure boiling. He introduced me to politics early, and there are many times I have regretted it, but the political circus in recent years has driven me away.

Every New Year's Day, Daddy would call me early to give New Year's greetings, and he enjoyed waking me up early with the call. I got him back one year when I had been out with girlfriends in Maryland. It must have been 1:30 am or so when I called to wish him a Happy New Year. He did not appreciate my laughter that time of the day.

In January or February of 1987, Daddy had some type of attack and ended up in the hospital. He was having difficulty breathing. It happened on a Sunday when it was raining and trying to sleet, and I had a bad tire on my car. My friend Sharon had just bought a Lincoln and offered me her car, insisting I go immediately. By the time I got on this side of the Potomac River Bridge, the roads were bad and there were so many gadgets on the dashboard of that Lincoln, I could not figure out anything. I had to stop at a gas station and ask how to turn on the windshield wipers. I made it to the hospital shortly after dark and Daddy was sitting on the side of the bed. I asked if he had eaten dinner, and he said they had brought him a bowl of homemade chicken soup. The only problem was the chicken must have run through the bowl and didn't stop, as he could not see one piece of meat in that bowl of soup. He still had his sense of humor. They treated him for bronchitis and released him a few days later.

I visited him at home that Friday after getting off work, and, again, Daddy was sitting on the side of the bed when I got there. I went in his room, sat beside him, wrapped my arm around him, and told him I was so happy and relieved that he was there and could not imagine what it would be like to come up that lane if he wasn't. He hugged me and implied that he loved me. That was the only time I ever heard those indications from him. Certainly, they must have told us we were loved when we were young children, as they surely gave us the impression that they loved us. I suppose we are not one of those mushy, mushy I-love-you tribes, but our actions speak louder than any words ever could.

On Saturday April 11, 1987, Daddy had been building a second barn since the home business was doing so well. He went in to eat lunch and watch his Saturday wrestling match. Terri was in the furniture barn with Mother where they were busy and had sold a large piece of furniture. Terrie went to get Daddy to help load it and found him lying across the end if the bed. She did CPR before the rescue squad arrived. The paramedics worked on him for forty-five minutes, to no avail.

Daddy had worked for People's Life Insurance Co, in the area and surrounding counties for years, and he knew a lot of people. His funeral was at Faulkner Bristow in Saluda, and the funeral procession drove Dad past Bob's Hole Road one more time. Mother had asked Esther Cook to ride in the lead car with her. Esther was a Black friend who worked for Mom and Dad at The Furniture Barn. Jennifer rode in the car with them and maybe Shannon. When they got the family seated under a tent at Windsor Gardens, I looked up to see the cemetery full of cars. They were lined all down the highway trying to gain entrance, and I was in total shock. Daddy was a very social guy and loved to talk. Thinking back, I doubt that he ever met a stranger, and he had left his signature locally.

I returned to Mother's a week after Dad's funeral, and I still remember the sickening empty feeling in my stomach as I drove up that lane. She had reopened her business and sitting there was a print from the living room wall that Daddy had bought many years ago, priced at $35.00. I bought the print in it's beautiful old frame. Many years before that, I was there one day when a pickup loaded with antiques came up the lane, and Daddy had bought the print for $10.00. It depicts a maiden who has taken her cattle to the creek for water. Research shows it was printed in 1906, and it hangs in my living room till this day.

If I were to reach an educated conclusion of what may have been an underlying issue with our parents, it would have been money, and Mother having to carry too many buckets of water. Daddy was a mechanic, and I doubt that he was paid a lot back then. I know he worked for Star Bakery in Crisfield for years, and they sponsored a race car. Daddy was the mechanic who kept that car running. He would take Wayne and me to the race tracks with him where we hung out in the pit when the cars were racing. I assume he kept the bakery's bread trucks running also. I remember once he came home with a steal splinter in his eye, and it had happened when he was changing a tire. The local doctor could not remove it, and late that night we went to a female doctor in Crisfield named Sarah Peyton. She was able to get the splinter out and save Daddy's eyesight.

Out of curiosity, I once again turn to the Federal Census and found that in 1940 both of our parents were listed as hospital employees in Baltimore City and married. Daddy had worked sixty-six hours the previous week and made $550 in the year of 1939. He was listed as an orderly and Mother was listed as a nurse's aide who worked only twenty weeks in 1939 and made $340. Either she was earning more money than Dad, or someone miscalculated. That was the year she graduated from high school, so she was only there a short time. Mother had worked forty-eight hours the week before. They were both listed as boarders, but I don't know if they were boarding at the hospital or in a private home.

The 1950 census was just released a couple of months ago, and it shows our parents living in Marumsco. Daddy was a mechanic at the bakery and had worked twenty-two hours the previous week, dated April 7, 1950. Salaries were not listed in that census, and Mother was not working at the time. I know we were living in Pocomoke when Phyllis was ready to crawl, but scooted instead. I know her toybox was loaded with baby rattles at Christmas. She was born November 16, 1951. So, it is safe to assume that Daddy left the bakery and went to work in Pocomoke shortly after the 1950 census was taken. Perhaps we were living there when Phyllis was born. Nevertheless, the move was better for the family, and I know Daddy was still working in Pocomoke when Hurricane Hazel hit in 1954. Maybe he worked there until they moved to Virginia. I do not know.

If Mother had not objected to Dad becoming a mortician, money might have flowed more freely than from a mechanic's wages. Dad used to get my attention with stories of a mortician's training at the hospital in Baltimore City. He told me that when they did an autopsy, they would cut the chest open with a meat cleaver and remove the organs. I had seen butchers use meat cleavers before, so that was a horror story in a child's mind. Once they removed all the organs, they stuffed the body with sawdust. He said to keep a dead person's eyes from opening, they put a penny under each eyelid, and to keep the mouth from hanging open, they sewed the lips together.

Speaking of Mom's objection to living in a funeral parlor and Dad being a mortician, I located his WWII draft card. He registered on October 16,

1940 in Baltimore City. They were living at 402 S. Bonsai Street, and he was employed at Bethlehem Steel Company at Sparrows Point in Baltimore City (we have a picture). He was six-foot-two and weighed 140 pounds. The point being that they got married in January and nine months later, he had a new job. There was no more mortician training, and Mom had called the shots.

The last time I looked at a deceased person, it was at my father's viewing, and I saw the stitches on his lips that he had told me about many years before. That was the vision I had of him in my mind for years. I have no intention of ever looking at anyone else who has passed away, instead choosing to remember them alive. Maybe Mom was right about that, after all. She used to talk about open caskets and the dead. She spoke about the people who would parade past a casket and talk about how good the deceased looked. In her words, "There never has been a dead person that looked good, and there never will be." I agree. She threatened to come back and haunt us if we had her casket open when she left this world, yet she refused to close Daddy's after I begged her to do at his viewing. Her response to me was, "Your daddy loved to socialize and talk to everyone he knew, and this is how he would have wanted it."

Mother was not known for her humor, but every once in a while, she would bring the house down with her dry sense of humor. She was not a huge fan of dogs and believed they were supposed to live outside. Daddy loved all dogs and especially his boxers. He had four, and they lived in the house. There was Deno, Missy, Brandy, and Lady. I do not recall which one was living when Daddy died, possibly Lady, but he was close to it. They were his four-legged children. He had a couple that would get into real dog fights, and I have seen them fight in the house turning over Mother's tables and breaking lamps. It was not a pretty sight. I saw two of them fight in the yard one day, and Daddy ended up sticking a broom handle in one of their mouths to break the grip. He finally made two muzzles out of chicken wire and turned them loose in the yard. Then they cut each other up with the stubs of the chicken wire.

At the time of Dad's death, I found a picture of his boxer at the house before we went to the viewing, and Wayne and Phyllis may have been in in it. I took the picture of his dog to the funeral home that night. After everyone had paid their respects and were sitting in the chapel pews, I took the picture out of my purse. I showed it to Mom and whispered in her ear that I wanted to put the picture in the pocket of Dad's suit jacket. Out of the blue and into the silence of a funeral parlor, she spoke very loudly, "I have a better idea. Why don't you put the *dog* in the casket with him?" Everyone in that chapel got a good laugh, and they were not quiet about it either. I have no clue what happened to that dog, but it wasn't there long after Daddy passed away.

Dad was very outgoing and likeable. He talked to anyone who would listen and told jokes, off-color by the standards of many. I'm not sure from where he inherited his sociable trait unless it was from his grandfather George, as Grover was not social when we were growing up, and Mom-Mom was shy and soft spoken.

There were times I thought Dad was cordial and kind to everyone in the world except those who lived under his roof. Often, he and I would butt heads. When I was young until way into my adult years, if I did something that he did not agree with, I would hear, "The road to hell was paved with good intentions." Oddly enough, the other quote that he repeatedly drilled into me was, "Good things come to all who wait," and when I was going through tough times, he would remind me. I asked him, more than once, how long one had to wait. Mother used to tell me that Dad and I butted heads often because I was just like him. Maybe she was right.

When I moved to Syringa with my parents, I met a girl who lived down the road by the name of Judy Copper whose family was heavy into the local church. Judy and I became friends, and she had local friends who were familiar with lots of different places, including the NCO club at Langley AFB. Her friend, Nelda, had a car, and we would go there with her but on one of those outings, her friend had too many drinks to drive us home. We made it to a pancake house or something close where Judy and I sat in the front seat of her car all night because Nelda was passed out in the backseat. Finally, she was convinced that she could drive, and I got home at 6:00 am. I took off my shoes, sneaked upstairs, and crawled in bed. Daddy gave me maybe thirty minutes before he started calling me. He did not let up until I came downstairs. I was trying to tell him what had happened and why I was out all night, but he did not believe me. He did not want to hear the B/S as he called it and responded with, "As long as you put your feet under my table and you sleep under my roof, you will do as I say." I was twenty-two or twenty-three years old at the time, and that is the way it was as he reminded me of the road to hell.

We all know that Dad loved cheddar cheese, his dogs, politics, car races, boxing, wrestling, and his Baltimore Orioles. He would snuggle into a chair close to the stove and listen to the games with a TV in the next room, and most of the time he would sleep through half of them. There's no question that he loved his family but was just a chip off the old block when it came to disciplining his children. It was the only way he knew because it was how he had been raised.

OUR ROCK AND OUR GLUE

I have said it many times and I will say it again, Mother was our rock. She was the glue, the nails, and the boards that held us all together. When we lost her on August 18, 2005, we lost our rock and glue. Had she not been the strong woman that she was, one could only wonder what would have happened to our family.

I do not remember her reading us bedtime stories or tucking us in at night, but I do remember those large paper storybooks that she read to me in the daytime.

There was a *Little Red Riding Hood* book, a *Mother Goose Nursery Rhymes* and *The Night Before Christmas* that both Wayne and I loved. Santa Claus' beard and Little Red Riding Hood's cape felt like velvet on the front of the books. Daddy had lots of books, and I am certain that reading to us at night was his job, since Mom worked nights. I don't know about my siblings, but she would sing with me and taught me that song "Puddin' Head Jones." For years, I thought she was singing about her family. "Puddin' Head Jones was fat and funny, and he didn't know beef from bones. That is why the kids all called him, Wooden Head, Puddin' Head Jones." There was also a page in our nursery rhyme book about "six and twenty blackbirds baked into a pie. When the pie was opened, the birds began to sing. Now wasn't that a dainty dish to set before the king?" On second thought, maybe it was a naughty dish to set before the king, I do not remember, but I would bug mother to sing it over and over.

When she was working at a nursing home in Marion Station, Mom wore a white starched uniform with a white hat, white shoes and stockings. I believe it was Mrs. Betts Nursing Home, and she would come home with stories to tell. The one I remember clearly was about some old man going nuts one night and jumping on the furniture. She said he was jumping up and down on the bed and grabbed the chandelier and started swinging like a monkey. She and Mrs. Betts could not get him down. Mrs. Betts called the police to get him down and into a straight jacket, and then they took him away. I remember her explaining to me what a straight jacket was. Sometimes she would take me there, or I would go with Dad to pick her up from work. It was a huge old Victorian house with pretty chandeliers in every room, and pretty sconces on the walls. The lights were on all over the house, and I looked at those lights many times in the evenings through the windows trying to see the old man swinging like a monkey.

Margaret Matthews

In the afternoons, Mom would try to nap, and I would sit on the floor next to her bed with books and crayons. There was a window there and always a cool breeze coming in. She would put Wayne in the crib and try to sleep before pulling another night shift, and I would keep talking to her as she was trying to sleep.

When I got a little older, she would talk about the patients at Baltimore City Hospital and how nasty and stinking some of them were when they got there. She, being an aide in training, had to bathe them and get them ready for surgery. She spoke of some of the women in labor and how dirty they were and how she had to shave them to prepare them for childbirth. She spoke of using hot witch hazel to treat those with hemorrhoids. She talked about the patients with open cuts and wounds. They used live leeches to eat the bacteria, and she said they would have to keep checking the patients to make sure the leeches stayed in place. If the leeches fell out of the sores, she had to gather them up and put them back where they belonged.

In the summertime, Mom picked up extra jobs helping not only Buddy Price, but also Bill Chaffey in his strawberry shanty. Her job was to weigh and count the berries as the farm laborers brought them in to be recorded. It had to be hot and miserable all day, but she worked right beside Mary Price and Helen Chaffey the entire season. One summer she stayed on and helped Mary Price in the shanty where acres upon acres of bell peppers were picked by the migrant workers.

Early in my childhood, Mom and Edna got a job working at Matthews Tomato Cannery (owned by Dad's cousin) that was located in Kingston, not far away. I remember Daddy driving the old car to pick them up from work, and Mary Jo and I would go with him. The buildings they worked in were nothing but large shanties with roofs and lots of tables and probably conveyer belts. There were smokestacks with smoke coming out of them everywhere, and at quitting time, a whistle would blow. It was hot sitting in the car, so we were always happy to hear the whistle blow. The place stunk almost as bad as the chum houses did from the tomatoes cooking. No doubt it was dirty work in a very hot environment. You could smell the cannery for miles down the road. I would bet that was probably one of the worst jobs that Mom ever had. I am not sure how she did it, but she did.

Later, Mother and Berky Price worked for Mrs. Paul's Kitchen that opened up in Crisfield. It was a seafood and packaging factory. Her friend Hazel Menzel worked there also, and the three of them rode to work together. There was a large old building between Marion and Crisfield where there was a bar and a dance floor. Mother had heard about incidents there with the sailors who would come from Chincoteague at nighttime and not have a ride back to the base. They would try to stop cars to catch a ride, and sure enough, one night some sailors laid down across the highway when they were on their way home. I don't remember if Mother or Berky was driving, but they decided they were not going to stop. They talked and laughed about the guys rolling and crawling across the highway to keep from getting hit by the car.

At one time, Mom worked for Perdue Chickens in Pocomoke City, and she complained about the smell in the processing plant. Maybe she worked there at nights. I was there once and saw all the naked chickens without heads swinging up high on a conveyer belt. It was a sight that would get a child's attention, for sure. She may not have worked there very long, but after that, she would not eat any store-bought chicken, but bought them directly from chicken farmers.

Mother stayed involved with the church the entire time she lived on the Eastern Shore, and she kept us involved. She saw to it that we got to go places and do things, even if we did wear hand-me-down clothes. My guess is that all kids wore hand-me-downs that were passed from family to family if they would fit someone's else kid. She bought us things that she probably could not afford, and more than likely did without herself. She made our Christmases something to remember for a lifetime, and even something as simple as a picnic, I'll never forgot.

Mother canned all summer long to stock the pantry. I recall one year her getting excited about going to the Vessey's house to pick apples. I got excited too, and she took me with her. When we arrived, I saw that they were crabapples, and I was so disappointed. I helped her by picking up the crabapples off the ground, and she took those things home and pickled them. She pickled a lot of things that I thought were weird but followed tradition from her childhood, no doubt. But the day came when she started cutting up watermelon rinds and pickled them. That's when I knew she was no longer sane. I learned later in life that watermelon rind pickles are well-known in the South. Her pickled beets were some of the best ever. She canned a lot of tomatoes, beans, and peaches and made jams and jellies to get through the winter months. She never stopped and must have been so worn out. I don't know if there was a crop issue or if things were going well financially, but I remember years later, her and Mary Price going to some food warehouse and buying canned vegetables by the case. They could get the dented cans at a discount, so that is what they bought. Maybe that was for things that were not grown locally.

We would go out to play in the wintertime and I would complain there was nothing good to eat. When we came in, she would have a large pot of beans with ham, hot biscuits, and a rice custard for dessert. It was delicious, and I remember to this day how good it tasted when we were half frozen from playing outside. There was never anything like sliced cheese, bologna, or sliced ham to make sandwiches back then. If one was to make a sandwich, it would have been eggs, peanut butter, or maybe a piece of ham left over from the one she cooked on Sunday. I do remember Mary Jo eating peanut butter and banana sandwiches, which I thought was weird.

My conclusion from all these memories is that there seemed to have been good times and bad ones. Maybe it depended on whether Daddy was working or not. Mother would fix chipped beef and gravy on toast every Saturday night for supper, and it was something we looked forward to. Then there were her potato cakes and corn fritters, and we kids would fight over the last one on the platter. We would rather have them than anything she put on the table. I ate just about everything she cooked, with the exception of liver and onions. I don't know if my siblings ate that, but Daddy loved it and Mother did too. Oh, and the codfish cakes. Yuck! Nothing ever smelled worse in that house than Mother cooking her codfish. Also on my list of dislikes was something in a can called hominy. It may have been corn, as Mother did not like grits, and she cooked it for breakfast. Her being from the South, it's strange that she did not eat grits or collards, nor did she sweeten her ice tea, thank God.

I remember clearly the smell from the coffee pot on cold winter mornings. When we would ask our parents if we could have some coffee, their response was "It will turn your skin dark." I am sure we questioned their answer and wanted proof, but they convinced all of us kids we did not want coffee. Consequently, none of us drank coffee, and I believe I am still the only one who does. It wasn't until I lived under the same roof with John McQueen, that I took up the habit.

Since Mother worked nights, she cooked our supper in the late afternoons, and I would have to get it on the table for the younger kids, then make sure they did their homework and took baths. Nothing disappointed me more than to get off the school bus and walk in to the smell of her cooking the codfish or a pot of cabbage. I did learn to eat cabbage later in life. To this day, probably my favorite recipes of hers were her sweet potato biscuits, rice pudding, and pickled beets. She may have taken a blue ribbon with her chicken and dumplings and fried chicken, as she was a good cook, to say the least. She grew up during the depression and knew how to make use of everything available at her fingertips to feed a family of six.

Mother would kill chickens and pluck the feathers by pouring hot water over them. Have you ever smelled a chicken that had hot water poured over it? Not good. I watched her and the other women pick up a chicken and twist it in circles until it's head came off, and someone had a chopping block made out of a tree trunk. That might have been at Roger Swift's and they would pick up a clucking hen and get her on the chopping block, and come down once with a hatchet. Whoever said the kids back then didn't know what violence was never witnessed that scenario...and there were concerns about the violence in cartoons. Funny.

One year, Mom must have killed all the chickens that we had in our yard, but there was still the big old handsome rooster that strutted around acting cocky, as roosters do. I remember Mother saying to him often, "You are going to be next if you are not careful." Times must have been bleak, as one day she killed the rooster and put him in the dinner pot. He was grass fed and tasted so much like wild onions no could not eat him. That damn strutting, cocky rooster died in vain.

I watched Mother pluck more chickens and clean more fish than I could count when I was a child, and somewhere along the way, I prayed those were two things I would never have to do to survive. It is a nasty job, and someone has to do it, but not me.

I was no stranger to the smell of chicken pens and chicken houses in the summertime. I knew what caused the smell, but you might not be a country kid unless you have experienced that unforgettable aroma.

Mother had her few chickens that lived in our backyard, scratching the dirt and clucking all day as chickens do. They actually hum or talk to each other in a dialogue that is very relaxing, and I love to listen to them. Those chickens had to do their business somewhere, and since they roamed the backyard, that was the spot. The grass was green and soft, and wearing shoes out to play was not on my list. Have you ever stepped in a pile of chicken poop and had it squish between your toes? I did more times than I can count, and the older I got, the less I liked it. When you step in chicken poop, you move quickly to back up, only there is another pile and it gets on the heel of your foot. Before you know it, your entire foot looks like someone has done a finger painting on the bottom. Once I realized that most piles of it had a white topping, I would learn to jump over the little piles that were white on top. There was only one problem. Not all of them were white, and you could not see them. They were probably left there by that darn rooster that no one in the family could eat. I will assure you of one thing: you cannot get chicken poop from between your toes by raking your foot on the grass, no matter how green and soft it is.

Mom told me that during the war they lived in Crisfield and were on food rations. Two of Daddy's uncles, Tom and Andrew Marshall, owned a crab shanty, and every night when they went home from Briddells, they would leave them soft crabs for dinner. Mother said because of the crabs and fresh veggies from family gardens, they did not suffer like many families did. They were living on Pear Street in Crisfield at the time.

I don't know where Mom got the old treadle sewing machine, but I don't think they got along very well. She did learn to embroider. I remember her buying the hoops, and I was fascinated by them. She would embroider tea towels and pillow cases, and she and her friends ordered the patterns from the newspapers. At one time she embroidered a set of dish towels with the seven days of chores on them, and they were pretty. I have a couple pillow cases that she did later on.

I also remember that she dragged us to someone's house in Westover or Kingston, and when I say drag, I mean drag. I have no clue who they were, nor did Mary Jo. I swear he was always dressed like the Amish. He had a long beard that went to his waist and wore a straw hat. He played the violin, and kept on playing the violin. We would be in their parlor and it was hot in there, and and they had no electricity. When the sun started going down, they lit their oil lamps. It was another one of Mother's torture chambers, and I hated it. You had to sit still and keep quiet and listen to the violin for what seemed like hours on end. It would take me many years of adult life to appreciate the music of a violin, if I ever did.

Mom's good friend and neighbor Mary Price's mother, lived on Somerset Avenue in Crisfield. Mary Price and Virginia Ward (the lady that took me to Ocean City in the summers) had a sister Sarah who lived in Marion. They would pick up Mother and all gather at the home in Crisfield. Sarah's daughter, Cookie Bradshaw, and I were in the same class. Her grandmother lived in a huge old Victorian home with a wrap-around porch, and there were blue hydrangeas planted all around the porch. Cookie and I were playing under those bushes one day when we spotted little orange things growing on a bush. We gathered a handful and started eating them. All of a sudden it was like our mouths were turning inside out and our tongues got in the way. We came out of those bushes screaming and running for help. We had eaten persimmons, and I guess you are not supposed to bite into them until after the frost has hit them. I have never touched them since even though I see them in the grocery stores now and then.

Mother spoke of their years living in Baltimore City and that Daddy chased every firetruck in the city to see where the fire was when he heard the sirens go off. One day the firetruck stopped, and he didn't. He ran into the back of the firetruck and totaled their car. You could hear the aggravation in her voice when Mom told the story many years later. She and Dad both talked about the white marble steps in the city, and how everyone scrubbed them to keep them clean. We have a photo of Aunt Thalia and her friend scrubbing the white marble steps in front of Mom and Dad's home in Baltimore City. I saw the marble steps when I lived in Maryland. Mom would talk about changing the curtains from winter to summer to keep the heat in or out, a practice she took to the Eastern Shore with her. She told me that Uncle Millard and Aunt Josie came twice to live with them when they had no money, and it was a struggle until Uncle Millard could find a job.

Josephine and Millard Daugherty
Courting Days - 1939
Taken in front of old Crisfield High School

Somewhere along Mother's journey she learned how to put home permanents in women's hair...and mine, I might add. There was a steady stream of neighbors who would come to the house, and Mother would put in what was known as Toni perms to make their hair curly. The perm solution would stink up the entire house, and the rollers looked like little bones. My third-grade school picture appears that I had one of those perms that was growing out. In the tenth grade, poodle hairstyles were the rage, so I got her to put one in at that time. I have the school picture. Mother could even perm her own hair, but a neighbor or Edna would roll the back for her.

Mother never liked living in Marumsco. She said that she had grown up poor, but she never knew what poor was until she moved onto the Matthews property. She disliked the low-lying area with all the standing water and the fact that there was no money to be made in the area. It was her opinion that the Matthews had money at one time, but Pop-Pop Grover had not worked, other than raising chickens and farming, since she had moved there. So if there had been money at one time, it was gone. She stated that he spent a lot of time sitting on the doorsteps trying to figure out how to bring lawsuits against others. I do recall a lawsuit about biddy chicks coming into the train station when it was hot, and a lot of them had died. They used to ship the biddy chicks in by the hundreds for him to raise and resell. He sued someone over that, and there was some story about strawberry shipments from the train station. Of course, he sued the contractors who did not tie down the house when the hurricane was approaching, which was justified. I have no inkling how any of that turned out for him.

That said, Mom and Pop-Pop were cordial to each other, and I never heard negative comments when I was a child. In fact, I remember the day she asked him for the old drop leaf table that was in the smokehouse, and he gave it to her. It was same table that had been painted green and that the eel dinner was served on. Mother stripped the paint off the table and it still sits in my living room. It is a Pembrooke table dating back to 1830 and made from Philippine mahogany. It belonged to Daddy's grandmother, Josephine Darby Matthews. However, she was not born until 1861, so it may have been her mother's.

Mother went into a panic shortly after Daddy died, worrying about money. She started selling off some of her old antiques and collectibles, and every time I returned from Maryland, items were already gone. She called me one day at work and said she was selling the table and asked if I wanted it. I agreed to buy it and the old Pierpoint lamp. She wanted $150 for both of them. Thank goodness she called me, and we still have the table. She had bought the lamp somewhere in her journey, and I had gone to Williamsburg Pottery with her and Daddy the day they bought the reproduction shade.

Some years ago, I shared with Mary Jo the stories that I had learned about Pop-Pop and how he treated Mom-Mom Amy and asked about her mother Edna and her father. The thing that stuck out in her mind was that she had seen her mother out there plowing the fields with the horse and plow while he sat on the step and watched. What we do know is that Daddy left Somerset County as soon as he turned twenty-one and headed for the city lights. The weekend after Mary Jo graduated from high school, she eloped and married a guy from Crisfield, so both of them were out of there. Allen Matthews was just thirteen years old when his father passed away.

There are indications that Grandpop George did well financially. Aunt Josie had gone to see her grandfather when he was in the hospital before his death. He told her that he had planned on leaving her something in his will, but when Grandmom Jo got sick, it took every penny they had saved. She died in 1934 and he lived until 1943. Then there were the toys that Daddy got for Christmas when he was a kid and it wasn't an orange and a few nuts in a stocking. There was George's engraved gold stopwatch with the horse, Dan Patches, on it from 1906 that Wayne inherited. Grandmom Jo had a wide gold wedding band with her initials on it, and Phyllis inherited that. Grandmom Jo, as Daddy called her, also had a gold chain bracelet with a disk that had her initials engraved. Grandpop George gave that to Aunt Josie when her grandmother died. I was told that Aunt Josie reached a point where she did not wear jewelry and was trying to sell the bracelet and that Daddy got upset about it. She did not sell it, and her daughter Kaye Daugherty, has the bracelet. I doubt any of those items were cheap at the time they were purchased. Then there is the hurricane lamp that was bought in 1906 according to Daddy, and surely it was a little pricey for the times. Not to mention all the fancy cars that Pop-Pop Grover owned. I don't know if he bought them or his parents.

Mother told me that she and Daddy had taken Grover to North Carolina with them one weekend to see her father after her mother died. While they were there, Grover needed to use the telephone, but her parents had never had a phone, so they took him to a neighbor's house to use their phone, and that is where he met Edna. Mother said they were going often, and the next time they went, Grover was sitting on Grandaddy Alex's front porch when they got to the house, and they were shocked. She said he stayed an entire week with her Dad one time and did not want to leave when they did. Obviously, his wheels were turning, and he was looking for a new bride.

I remember numerous times of Mother talking to others that she feared her kids would get Rocky Mountain Spotted Fever. I did not know what she was talking about, and she was not living when I was diagnosed with it. It was probably a common childhood disease at that time.

There were wild blueberry bushes growing all along the woods on the Road to Frog Eye, and I loved blueberries. When I got a little older and Mom was home in the evenings, she would let me walk the road to pluck and eat the blueberries. So, one evening I was strolling along plucking away when a white snake dropped out of a pine tree right in front of me. I was out of there and they heard me coming home. I did not know snakes laid around in trees, and I sure didn't know there was such a thing as a white snake. That was the end of the blueberry excursions. I decided that snake could have every one of them. That was one of only four snakes I encountered when I was growing up, and that was four too many.

Mom saved green stamps, as did most women of the day, and I remember clearly the set of dishes in the A&P grocery store that she set her eye on to earn with her green stamps. The dishes were white and had a burgundy berry and greenish ivy pattern on them. For every dollar you spent at the grocery store, you would get green stamps, and once you had enough to fill your book, you could purchase a dish with them. She got her set of dishes, and she also got a tall white lamp with green ivy painted around the base. If I am not mistaken, that is the lamp that was broken when Dad's boxers turned her table over at the house in Virginia.

After we settled back in Deltaville, I started messing around a little with the Matthews genealogy and found some information regarding Daddy's grandmother, Josephine Darby Matthews. I was at Mother's and mentioned I had found information on Dad's grandmother, and she responded, "She wasn't your father's grandmother. She was mine." I froze in my tracks and reminded her that Josephine Darby had raised Daddy. She came back at me with, "Well, how come her picture hung on our dining room wall the entire time I was growing up?"

I was stunned, and didn't know what to think or say, so I tried to make a joke out of it, "Well, no damn reason. We all do stupid things, we were inbred." Whoever was there laughed, including Mother, but I knew I had waited too late to discuss the family history with her. She had been having TIAs off and on.

I only had a couple disagreements with our Mother, and the first one I remember was regarding Geraldine Wake at the house in Syringa, and if I am not mistaken, I was twenty-one years old. It was spring or summer, and Geraldine was there cleaning, and I was upstairs helping her clean. Mom was downstairs putting her noon-time dinner meal together: butter beans, fried chicken, sliced tomatoes, or whatever she cooked that day and that famous ice tea of hers.

She called me to come and eat, so I went down and asked, "What about Geraldine?" She replied that Geraldine could eat after we were finished. I picked up a glass of ice tea because I was hot and thirsty, and said, "Mother, you have had Black ladies helping you since I was a child, and Geraldine has been here for years. They have cooked for us, babysat us kids, and cleaned the houses. Geraldine is upstairs in the heat scrubbing woodwork and windows. Why can't she sit at the table and eat with us?"

Mother was raised in the South and it was what she had been taught as a child. I do not recall what happened that day, but later Geraldine got sick and had to quit cleaning. I remember we took food to her house when she was down sick. I know the day Daddy was buried, Ester Cook (another local Black lady) rode in the limousine with Mother at Mother's request, and if I am not mistaken, she sat next to Mother under the tent. Ester worked for Mom and Dad in The Furniture Barn and continued on with Mother after Daddy passed away. I gave Mother a surprise birthday party a couple years before she passed away, and Ester Cook attended the party that Sunday afternoon.

I will never know what happened early on with my parents, and it doesn't matter, but what matters is that they managed to keep us all together. My thoughts are that Dad had no defense or I would have heard the story. I suppose while he was in Baltimore chasing firetrucks, she was working in Somerset County, and Mom being the new girl in town with dark curly hair and big brown eyes, she was being chased. Just maybe she was firing a warning shot over the bow to let Daddy know he had better get those feet on solid ground.

We never went to bed hungry or cold, were bathed, and wore clean and ironed clothes every day. Wayne and I can attest to the fact that we got more medical attention than we wished for. We were raised in church, taught to respect others, and to carry our own buckets of water, and we were loved by both parents. Mom never quit giving, not only to family, but to those in need, and she showed all of us where her heart was every day of her life until she had that second stroke in 2005.

Mother managed to rough it out on the Eastern Shore for eighteen years, and we have no idea of how many cloudy days she went through to do it. She was happy when they moved to Virginia, and I know she was glad to get out of Somerset County—still the poorest county in the state of Maryland. It was after moving to Middlesex County that she picked up her nursing and did private duty for years, giving it up sometime after Glen's accident.

When Daddy passed away in 1987, our parents had been married for forty-seven years, managing to overcome hurdles like so many others, no doubt. Every year for their anniversary on January 14, I would send them a bouquet of long-stemmed red carnations. I have the vase that Mom used to put them in. The year after Daddy died, I sent Mom a teacup arrangement with little pink roses on January 14 and promptly received a phone call. "Why did you send flowers?" she asked. I tried to explain that I did not want to send the red carnations but didn't want her to think I had forgotten it was January 14th. She reminded me that Daddy was gone, and she no longer had an anniversary. Her words were loud and clear. They spoke volumes, and I listened.

I was headed to Deltaville one weekend during the summer and stopped in the see Mom and Glen. It was around dinnertime, and they were eating what I thought to be an odd combination. It was something like boiled eggs and broccoli. When she mentioned the menu, she said she was tired of cooking. Indeed, she was, and had done her time for many a year cooking for the rest of us meals that we will never forget.

Mother's granddaughter, Jennifer Jenkins, Phyllis' daughter, decided to write and print a cookbook dedicated to Mother and her delicious recipes. She spent countless hours going over recipes with Mother and gave every family member a copy of the book for Christmas. She titled the book *Nanny Crocker*, and it is a gift that each of us will always cherish. The first thing I went for was the recipe for Mother's sweet potato biscuits. I flubbed them up big time.

When the family moved to Virginia, they lived in Dr. Fleet's home

Old Fleet Place in Syringa, VA where Margaret and Lake lived when they first moved to Virginia.

on Regent Road, but within a year or so, they bought the old Revere home from Mrs. Mears in Syringa. It was a huge house that had been built prior to the Civil War, and one that needed work. They borrowed enough money to put in plumbing and a bathroom. If memory serves me right, the total loan was for $3700.00 and Daddy had a coupon book with payments of $37.50 a month. He would show me how many coupons were still left in the book and how they were dwindling. My parents did what they could to update the house, and I remember Daddy tearing down plaster and putting up drywall in the dining room. He built a long-arm tool to hold the drywall to the ceilings, and Wayne and I would have to steady the tool while he did the nailing. They painted and papered and made it livable, and the work went on for years. They painted the exterior and the old wooden shutters that were so grand, tore down walls, opening up rooms, got rid of the dozens of doors, and installed a new heating system.

It was there that Mother seemed the happiest. The dining room table was always pretty and loaded with beautiful china dishes, delicious food, and dinner guests abounded. Holiday meals were adorned with her pickled pears, chow chow, and homemade bread and butter pickles served in the various antique dishes that she had collected over the years. She started on her bread dough the night before and always served homemade yeast rolls. It was at that table that John McQueen saw his first platter of fried oysters during Christmas dinner, and he ate them.

I would visit before the holidays and sit there with Mother and polish all the silver, This tradition went on for years and is one job that I still do, remembering those nights spent at the kitchen table with Mother. The Christmas trees were always big and Daddy still cut them from the woods.

I recall one year the tree he brought home was so scraggly looking that Mother insisted he take it down and get another one...and he did. When we would all get there on Christmas Eve and unload the vehicles, the gifts filled the entire living room floor. Daddy would get all emotional, and the tears would flow as he spoke of how blessed our family was.

However, it was not a Hallmark Christmas every year at the Matthews home. Such was the year Dad waited late to shop, and bought two bed pillows for Mother for Christmas. He obviously had someone else wrap them for him, and when mother opened them, he told her one of them was for him. That was not a memorable Christmas Eve (or maybe it was) but he might have learned his lesson, since, from then on, he shopped at the ladies dress shop in Urbanna and had the owner choose Mother's gifts.

Just has she had always done for the holidays, Mother would start buying her ingredients early to bake her cakes and cookies. The candied fruits and nuts for her fruitcakes were expensive, and sometimes she could not find what she was looking for, so she did not wait until the last minute. Besides, the fruitcakes had to sit for weeks to soak in whatever type of bourbon that she poured on top of them. Her circle of friends only got larger in Virginia, so one year she baked a lot of applesauce cakes and fruitcakes. She wrapped them in tinfoil and stored them in a room that was not heated.

Mother and I made a quick trip to Newport News one very cold afternoon right before Christmas to pick up an electric train from Montgomery Ward for Steve. It was our intention to jog right down there and come back before the kids got home from school. We managed to beat the bus home, but when we went in the door, we saw scraps of tinfoil scattered from the kitchen door all the way through the house.

Dad's two boxers had managed to get in that end bedroom and had torn into every cake, which must have been eight or nine cakes. They had eaten all of some and just taken several bites out of the rest and there were piles of broken cakes and tin foil covering a pathway from the bedroom to the kitchen door. Mother broke down crying. Christmas was almost there, and there wasn't enough time for her to start over. The cakes were her gifts for family and friends, and she had put a lot of time and money into them. The spirit of Christmas had gone out the door for anyone within earshot. Daddy was praying that his dogs would not get sick and die from the bourbon, nuts and fruit, and she was praying they did. If there is one thing for certain, it is that Daddy did not enjoy Christmas that year.

Mom and Dad's house was home to Wayne, Phyllis, Glen and me when we were there. It was home to my children and some of the other grandchildren, and great memories were made there for the entire family. My siblings always had friends over, and I brought my friends to visit. Mother and Dad had a lot of company from the Eastern Shore, as well as family from out of state.

Everyone adjusted to the new area and made new friends. I was invited to a get-together at someone's home one night and had taken a seat in the living room where I set my purse beside the chair. There may have been a dozen people. There was a lot of food and laughs that night, and one of my girlfriends brought me back home.

The next day, I went in my wallet and did not have one single cent to my name. I had only gone to the bathroom once and left my purse sitting beside the chair. But who would do this? I had known a few people who were present, and I was hysterical that someone would steal every dollar I had worked for the week before. I was honest, and people did not steal from others where we came from. Mother and Dad tried to console me, saying, "Just because I did not steal did not mean that others would not steal from me out there in this great big world." Daddy reminded me that morning that the road to hell was paved with good intentions, but I didn't see how it applied to my situation.

Obviously, I was still a country girl, gullible and naïve. On another occasion, Mother and I had taken the kids shopping in a clothing store in Mathews County. I had picked out summer clothes for the children and when I went to pay, my wallet was not in my purse. I went out and searched in the car but did not find it. I was certain I had it when we left home. I told the owner what the problem was and that I would look for it when I got home. She asked for my name and phone number. The wallet was not to be found, and as it turned out, she happened to know a woman who was in the store at the same time. She called the sheriff, who went to the woman's house where my wallet was retrieved. The woman was arrested, and they called for me to come and press charges, but I did not do it, so I'm not sure whatever happened. Apparently, when I was struggling and trying clothes on the kids, she reached in my purse and took the wallet.

Somewhere along the way, Mother decided to collect irises and planted them everywhere. I believe she was collecting them from a private home in Ware Neck where she worked as a nurse. She had a lot of different varieties and colors. She brought home lilac bushes and peonies, and Dad planted tulip beds that were beautiful in the spring, so they were making up for lost time on the Eastern Shore. We bought Mother a pink dogwood tree for Mother's Day that still blooms every year. I dug up a couple of the lilac shoots from under her bushes one rainy Sunday afternoon when I was there. It was after she had fallen and cracked her backbone for the second time. Some type of blight killed all three of them about two years ago. The peonies and irises that I brought home still bloom, though, and Wayne has a few of them too.

I thought for a long time the old place on the hill was haunted. I went to visit Mom and Dad the first winter they were there and only had Steve at the time. It was cold and snowing, and there was a vent in the kitchen ceiling which let the heat rise to the bedroom above. Steve and I slept in that room, as he was a toddler. In the middle of the night, something started banging on the window right next to the bed, and I could not see anything out the window. I finally grabbed Steve and ran downstairs with him, only when I got to the bottom of the stairs there was another hallway with five or six doors. I was frantically opening doors looking for Dad to no avail. I was lost in my parents' house. Finally, when I opened the last door, a black cat jumped up three feet in the air and screeched, and I must have jumped two feet and hollered. I don't know who scared whom the most, but apparently, he had been huddled up close to the front door to get out of the snow. The next day, Dad went out and saw that one of the wooden shutters upstairs had blown loose from the top and the wind was banging it against the house.

On another occasion, Dad was delivering papers for the Richmond or Newport News paper and Mother worked nights. I had moved back home with my children, and Dad would leave home about 4:30 in the morning for the paper delivery. It was springtime, and all the windows were open. Every morning when he left, someone would walk across the front porch, back and forth. It was dark, and again I could not see anything in front of the windows. Mom and Dad thought I was nuts, but I knew what I was hearing. My siblings were young at the time.

This must have gone on for days, so one morning Daddy sat in the living room waiting to hear the intruder, and, sure enough, it happened again. He yanked the front door open, probably with his gun in hand, and Bam! There in front of him was a huge dog—I believe a boxer—pacing the front porch. The dog belonged to Mrs. Mears who lived out the lane. So, the only ghosts that were ever found were four-legged ones.

They might not have had ghosts, but snakes seemed to be plentiful at their house. More than likely, they resided there when before Mom and Dad moved in. There were several locust trees that had rotted in the center, and Daddy said they were living in the centers of the rotten trees. After Glen's accident, he became somewhat of a bird watcher and was always thrilled when a woodpecker would come to peck on the pecan tree. Someone had hung a huge birdhouse in the circle where Glen could see it from the kitchen window, and Mother had been told a story about a snake getting into somebody's birdhouse to get the baby birds. Forget that nonsense, she decided, and had someone remove all the birdhouses. Glen's bird watching days were history.

A man who lived up the county by the name of John Lane painted for Mom here and there. John Lane brought his wife and teenage son down to The Furniture Barn to see Mom, and the huge birdhouse that used to hang in the circle was sitting outside the barn. He liked it, and Mother told him to take it with him. He owned a rather large old station wagon, so the birdhouse fitted in the back.

It was just getting dark when the Lanes left and headed home. When they got in front of the old grocery store in Locust Hill, something started crawling across the top of the backseat where their son was sitting. He screamed, "Snake, stop, stop!" John Lane hit the brakes, stopped in the middle of the highway, and everyone jumped out. He left the car running and the lights on. It turned out to be a six-foot black snake that had curled up in that birdhouse and must have been curious about where he was going on a Saturday night. The story goes that John Lane, his wife, and son were jumping up and down screaming and acting crazy in the middle of the highway. Cars stopped and people gathered. Someone went somewhere and called the sheriff's office. I do not know who recovered the car, nor the snake, but I can still see Mother telling that story. I seldom saw her laugh any harder than when she repeated it.

In 1998, the family was weighed down with another crisis. I came to Virginia for a couple days and was staying at Mother's. I was overwhelmed and did not know which way to turn or what the answers were. Unknown to anyone, I got in my car and went to the cemetery to talk to Dad. I was late getting back, and dinner was waiting for me. Mother asked where I had been and I told her I went and talked to Daddy and asked him what I should do. She looked at me, sat in the kitchen chair and said, "Well if he answered you, I am packing my bags and leaving here tonight." Daddy had been deceased eleven years at this point, and there was that dry sense of humor that Mother rarely showed. Perhaps she was serious.

On the 11th of June 2004, the aide that we hired walked in the house that morning to find Mother sitting on the side of her bed unable to talk. She called me immediately, and I told her to call 911, that I was on my way. Mother spent a few days in the hospital, regained her speech, and the doctor said she had suffered a mini stroke, probably from sleeping the wrong way on her neck. She seemed to recover quickly, and John and I took her and Glen to the Fourth of July parade in Deltaville. The day was so hot my head was soaked from sweating. Mom claimed that was the first parade she had ever attended. I think she had just forgotten. All I wanted to do was get into the air conditioning and cool off. I was going to cook dinner that evening for them. All Mother wanted to do was sit on the hot porch and eat ice cream, so that is what we did.

The following year on June 15, 2005—Rachel's eleventh birthday—Mother had another stroke. Terrie was living in the house with her and caught a glimpse of her sitting in the living room early in the morning. When she approached Mother, once again, she could not speak. Terrie said when the rescue squad was loading Mother in the ambulance, she saw tears running down her cheeks. We were not so lucky that time, but at least Phyllis was home with us. The doctors kept doing brain scans and showed us what was happening. She could not speak nor could she swallow. They were sending her to a nursing home to recover. She was sitting on the bedside when I told her we were going to West Point for three weeks of rehabilitation, and she seemed to understand. Something happened between the hospital and the nursing home, and when we saw her, she had taken another turn backward and was never the same again.

Phyllis, Wayne, and myself or the grandkids were in there with her off and on all day and night, and we took Glen to visit her. Wayne worked close to the nursing home and would stop by early in the mornings and in the evenings. One night, he went and found her bed empty, so he left her room. When he got to the lobby, he heard some moaning, and there was Mother facing the wall in the corner of the lobby all by herself. She had been forgotten by staff and left there alone. Lord knows how long she would have sat there had he not discovered her. God only knows what he thought when he saw the empty bed.

Phyllis had to fly back to Mississippi on August 14 to sign tax papers, and I was on my way to the nursing home on August 15 when Phyllis called me. I told her that it had been two months since Mother's stroke and the situation was just horrible. Her response was, "Do you know what will be even worse than this? If we are still going through this six month's from now." She was right.

Mother did not recognize any of us, and Glen would get so upset trying to talk to her that we had to stop taking him to visit. In the meantime, Phyllis got Glen into a nursing home, and it was his choice. He was optimistic that someone would teach him how to walk again.

The staff asked me to bring things that Mother was familiar with and things that had scents she might recognize. She used Ponds face cream for years, so I took that, and bought a slice of lemon meringue pie and a cucumber. She responded to none of it, not even when I tried to put a small amount of pie filling on her lips. She would just stare at the ceiling. This is hard to relive. The only response I ever got was when I took lotion and would rub her legs with it in the evening. She seemed to smile slightly, and I could tell she enjoyed it. A nurse came in and ordered me not to do it anymore, as she might have a blood clot and that could break loose. I have thought about that often and wondered what difference it made at that point. I have regretted not continuing the rub-down on her legs every night.

Mother lived for sixty days and passed away on August 18, 2005. Phyllis was here all summer with us, with the exception of a couple days. Her husband and daughter drove from Mississippi, and the entire family gathered to go and tell Glen that Mother was gone. He refused to leave the facility he was in and come back to the house that night. I approached his nurse and told her we had lost our mother, that we had told Glen, and he did not want to go home. I asked her if they could keep an eye on him and if he were to break down to call us. Her response was "I don't have time to babysit." It took me a while to absorb her curt response, but I decided she was a bitch who had no business wearing a nurse's badge. Terrie went early the next morning and told Glen it was time to come home, and he did. The problems across the river only got worse as time went on.

It would be almost two years before we would move Glen to a facility in Middlesex County. It wasn't as fancy as where he was originally. There were no mahogany Queen Ann chairs in the dining room, and the curtains were simple little tie-backs, not custom-made swags, but the personal attention was a hundred percent better and he was known by so many people in the county. He seemed to be happy and content there. He was not sick but handicapped. He spent the last two years of his life just up the road from where he had grown up. In this case that old saying, "All that glitters is not gold" was very true.

Margaret Cline Jones Matthews
Early 1940's
Baltimore City, MD

A Broken Heart We could not Mend

That Christmas, four months after Mother's death, Wayne went to pick up Glen on Christmas Eve morning. He spent the day and Wayne brought him here that evening. We could not take him to Mother's house as everything had been stolen on Thanksgiving. When he came in, he saw the old Matthews hurricane lamp lit in the dining room and let me know it was his. I told him I was keeping it safe so nothing would happen to it, and he agreed.

We ate Christmas brunch, and after that, I put Glen in the car to go to the cemetery. I had two live green wreaths with large red bows to put on our parents' graves, and he saw me load them in the back of the vehicle. When I got into the car, he grabbed my arm and kept holding up two fingers. I pretended I did not know what he was talking about. By the time we got to the Get-'n-Zip, he was still tugging on my arm, and I told him to write down what he was trying to say. He scribbled three letters on his little tablet, "MOM" and I had to tell him again that yes, she had gone to heaven with Daddy." When I got to the cemetery he was bawling and it was killing me inside, so I pulled the car over and hoped he could not see me putting the wreaths on the graves, but he did.

We left immediately and went to Wayne's house, but no one was there, so I took him to Clarence Sprouse's house. Wayne had located Clarence and helped to arrange for him to live on the property to help Mother and Glen after Daddy had passed away. He had lived on the property for years as a caretaker. We would have never made it without him. Clarence finally got him to quit bawling and settle down a little.

Speaking of Clarence and Glen, another incident just came to mind regarding the two of them. Hurricane Isabelle had gone through here a week or so before and no one had any power. Of course, there is no water if the pumps could not run, and the National Guard came to Deltaville with trucks loaded with bottled water. I called Mother to tell her to send Clarence and Glen to get water as there were limits on how much I could get. She told me that Clarence had driven Glen to Deltaville just to get out and see the damage here. I informed her that the National Guard was in front of the Community Center and there was a sign out there for free water, and she started laughing. She said, "They will not come back here with water because Glen cannot talk, and Clarence cannot read." They went home without water.

It was months later when Glen entered into a physical therapy program at the nursing home, and he was encouraged that he would learn to walk again. I went to visit him one afternoon after is PT class and we talked about his progress. He wanted Mother to come and see how much better his leg was and how strong he was getting. He wanted me to tell her to come to see him. So, I realized, once again, that he had not accepted the fact that we had lost her.

A few months before Glen passed away, I was at the nursing home and Glen was trying to tell me something. He would take that hand and wobble it like he was walking with a cane, which represented Mother walking. He started telling me that Mother had been there to see him the night before. He kept pointing up and then the wobbling motion would begin, and I asked him if Mother had been there with him and he said, "Yes." Who was I to argue that she wasn't? Mother used to tell me that God would take Glen before he took her so she did not have to worry about him. That was not the case, but he went to join them one day short of the fifth anniversary of our mother's death.

Glen started getting choked while eating the simplest things like scrambled eggs and cantaloupe. Tests were ordered and on July 31, 2010 he was diagnosed with cancer of the esophagus. The doctor brought out the film and said it was the largest cancer in the throat that he had ever seen and that the accident was going to get him in the end because of the crushed diaphragm. The only option available was to cut a slit in his throat below the tumor and feed him through a tube. He said Glen might live six months with the procedure and without it probably only weeks. We decided that he had been through enough in his lifetime and dismissed the option. They ordered morphine to make him more comfortable if needed. He may have had one dose and refused the rest.

I had gotten up early on August 17 and was sitting on the deck with a cup of coffee at 7:30 am when something told me I needed to go talk to Glen right then. When I got there, an aide and a custodian were in the room, and I asked them to give us some private time. When I closed the door, Glen and I talked, and he seemed more coherent than usual. Possibly it was because they had taken him off his normal medications. I asked him if he was ready to go, and he did not know. I told him it should not be this way, as I was the oldest. We talked about Mom and Dad, Mom-Mom Amy and the rest of the family. He acknowledged they were all in heaven. We discussed the kids in the family and how much they loved him. He referenced his rubbing their heads when they were babies in the bed with him from Jennifer and Shannon to the latest, Hannah who was Frankie and Crystal's daughter. He had seen them just two days before. Most of the kids in the family visited him that week, and I took Natalie and Ethan who entertained him with his bird collection and each bird's call.

We laughed about things he had done in his childhood. Strangely, he kept his eyes closed most of the time except when he laughed or looked at his watch, which he did repeatedly. I told him how much each of us loved him and how deeply he would be missed. I gave him messages to deliver and he gave me a thumbs up. When I started to leave, he motioned for me to close the window blinds, so perhaps his eyes were bothering him and that's why he kept them closed.

It was the most difficult conversation I have had in my life, but I managed to hold myself together the entire time. That is, until I got outside the building and sat on the wooden swing in the yard.

That afternoon, Rachel and I went shopping to buy Glen a new outfit, which included a baby-blue dress shirt to match his blue eyes. We went to Mizpah to see him about 2:30 that afternoon and he was sleeping. I said "Glen, look who came to visit you." He opened his eyes and smiled at Rachel. They had a brief conversation but he wanted to sleep. I decided I would return that evening.

Both of my daughters were working at Mizpah at the time and Timmy called me at 6:30 to tell me Rachel had just been in the room with Glen before leaving work, and it wasn't necessary that I go that evening. He was resting well, and she had turned him on his other side, but he kept looking at his watch. My sister had just flown back to Mississippi that day to take care of some business. The phone rang at 7:35 pm and the nurse told me that an aide had just gone into Glen's room and he was gone. I called Terrie who was on the way back from Kilmarnock and was there within minutes. She recommended that I not go up there. I called my brother and he decided not to go either. It had been seventeen days since Glen's diagnosis. My sister and I stayed on the phone off and on all night, and she took the first flight that was available back to Virginia the next morning.

All day, Glen had kept checking his watch like he was expecting someone or had to be somewhere at a certain time. Just maybe Mother told him what time she would be there to get him. I, for one, would not argue against that theory.

Someone took Glen's new clothes to the funeral home—probably Phyllis—and I sent a tie tack that had belonged to Daddy. It was a star with a diamond chip in it. The funeral home called me and said that it is not standard practice to bury individuals with jewelry, and they wanted to return his watch and the tie tack. I told them, "No. Let them go with him."

Glen lived to be fifty-seven years old and progressed so much further than the doctors ever gave one hint of hope that he would. Everyone noticed how good natured he was and how he was always smiling and friendly in spite of his disabilities. He loved all the kids in the family, his food, his wrestling, and his Baltimore Orioles just like Daddy did.

NOTES FROM DADDY*

*Information given by Lake Siddell Matthews to me in the 1980s regarding the Matthews family history. Thank God, I scribbled them all down.

Lake Matthews and Margaret Cline Jones Matthews Married in Baltimore City, MD on January 14, 1940. I do not believe this was taken on that day as mother has her jacket off. They met there in 1939 and moved to the Eastern Shore in June, 1943.

L ake (my father) was born on his mother's birthday October 5, 1916 on the Matthews farm. He attended the one-room school in Marumsco for six years. The school was approximately two miles from the farm.

His grandfather, George Alfred Matthews, hitched up the wagon and horse every day and carried him to the schoolhouse and then went back each afternoon and picked him up. Every Saturday, his grandfather gave him a nickel, hooked the horses to the wagon, and took Daddy to the store to buy candy.

When Dad was thirteen years old, he was diagnosed with TB in his lungs. He was cured from the disease but it kept him out of the service when WWII broke out. His middle name, Siddell, came from a doctor who had treated his father, Grover, at Mt. Wilson Hospital. When Grover was in his early thirties, he was diagnosed with TB and was in a sanitorium.

Aunt Josie (Dad's sister) told me that Dr. George Coulbourne wanted Daddy to go to a hospital in Baltimore to get treatments for his lungs when he was a teenager but that Pop-Pop would not agree to it. He insisted he needed him to stay there on the farm to work.

Lake Siddell Matthews graduated from Marion High School on May 29, 1935 in Somerset County, MD. He lived on the farm in Marumsco with his family until October 1937 when he turned twenty-one. He was supposed to get married on his birthday, October 5, but his girlfriend called off the wedding. He left Somerset County and went to work for City Hospital in Baltimore City cleaning, painting, and doing handiwork while studying to be a mortician. He met Mother at City Hospital in April 1939. She had sailed on the Old Bay Liner from Norfolk, Virginia to Baltimore City with a close friend, Mary Lee Sawyer. The two of them were born and raised in Pasquotank County, N.C. Both graduated from Newland High School in May 1939 and traveled to Baltimore to enter nurse's training.

I wished I had asked him who he had been engaged to, but thank goodness the marriage didn't happen. Had he married a local girl, we would have been stuck on a farm somewhere in Somerset County.

Margaret and Lake were married January 14, 1940 at Patterson Park Parsonage in Baltimore City. Dad left the hospital and went to work at Bethlehem Steel at Sparrows Point and worked at Glen L. Martin during the war. They rented an apartment over a High's Store in the city. Dad worked at Glen L. Martin Company in Baltimore City during World War II. He and Mom moved back and forth to the Eastern Shore numerous times and made their final move there in April 1943. It was there they had four children.

Lake and Margaret lived in Somerset County (Marumsco area) until they moved to Syringa, Virginia April 23, 1960.

Lake's sister, Josephine Mahala Matthews, was born on February 2, 1924 on the Matthews farm. Lake was seven years old when his mother Amy and sister Josephine (five months old) moved to Crisfield. They lived with Amy's father, John Marshall, and then Aunt Agnes Hoffman. Dad stayed on the Matthews farm and was raised by his grandparents, Josephine

Darby and George A. Matthews. Josephine was named after both her paternal and maternal grandmothers.

Dad and Josie's mother was Amy Gertrude Marshall (Mom-Mom Amy) born on October 5, 1890 on Smith Island, Maryland. She was the daughter of John Marshall and Mahala Thomas Marshall, next to the youngest of thirteen children. Amy was very young when her mother died. She was raised in the Baptist Church and converted to Church of God in the 1930s.

Amy married Grover A. Matthews on August 9, 1910, and they had four children. One child was stillborn and buried at Rehobeth Baptist Church in Somerset County. Another was born dead and is buried on a plot on the Matthews property in Marumsco, MD. Both of the children were boys born sometime between 1910 and 1916 before Dad's birth. Amy died from stomach cancer on April 15, 1975 at the home of her daughter, Josephine Mahala Matthews Daugherty, in Delaware. She is buried at the cemetery in Crisfield, Maryland on Chesapeake Avenue next to her sister, Agnes Pearl Hoffman.

When Mom-Mom Amy filled out Aunt Josie's birth certificate, she stated that she had one stillborn child. A short time before she passed away, she made the statement to Aunt Josie and Kirk, "Oh look, there is the Lord, and he is holding my baby." Kaye Daugherty (cousin) and I discussed this, and she always heard that Mom-Mom lost two children. We concluded the other loss was more than likely a miscarriage. Kaye recently informed me that the baby she lost was named George, no doubt after Grover's father. I had never heard that the child had been named.

Dad and Josie's father was Grover Allen Matthews born August 27, 1888 at Tull's Corner (I believe this was at Marion Station). He attended school through the eighth or ninth grade. He was a farmer and a carpenter who built the two-story house on the back of the farm where I was born. Grover also worked for the state of Maryland, dragging the roads with a horse-drawn road grader. The house he built was moved to the front of the property on the road before Wayne was born.

Grover had TB in his early thirties and was treated at Mt. Wilson sanitorium. Pop-Pop Grover was drafted during World War I in 1918. He was to leave Somerset County on November 15, but the war ended on

November 11, so he did not have to go.

He was a car addict and owned a new 1922 Maxwell, a new 1923 Hup mobile, a new 1924 Star, a new 1927 model T Ford and a new1929 Plymouth. Amy left him in 1924.

Grandpop George (as Dad called him) and his wife, Josephine, bought the Matthews farm on the Road to Frog Eye in 1901. Grandpop George was a farmer who had a good disposition and loved everybody, but George drank a little whiskey and had a mean streak in him if he overdid it. However, his favorite beverage was cold coffee and he was always drinking it. He was an animal lover who kept his horses and cattle very fat. George was an early riser getting up at 5:00 am every day and was a great boxer in his younger days. He was a good farmer who grew a large garden in which he enjoyed working.

Grover A. Matthews and second wife Edna Jones - 1941

Grover was married the second time to Edna Jones of Pasquotank County, NC in the early 1940s. She and Margaret (Mom) were not related. Edna had a young son named David and she and David came to Maryland on the bus. Grover and Edna had two children: Mary Jo Matthews, born April 20, 1944 and George Allen Matthews, born January 19, 1950.

Daddy had told me years ago that either his grandfather George or Charlie Smith came in the house drunk one night and drank a quart of vinegar thinking it was ice tea. On another occasion, one of them went into the ice box one night after drinking and drank an entire quart of clabber that was always kept to make biscuits.

George came home one day with a young Black boy about five years old. No one ever knew who the child was or where he came from. The family was told that his name was Charlie Smith. He was there to stay and grew up on the Matthews farm where he worked the farmland. He lived there until Grover and Edna married in the early '40s, at which time he moved to a house a short distance down the road. Charlie got sick, and Mother and Edna took care of him until his death. He was buried at Frog Eye Church. Mother said that she and Edna went to his funeral, and they were the only white folks there. She had taken me with her and I cried so loud, she had to stand outside with me until the service was over.

*There was a photo of Charlie Smith with the horse and plow in the drawer at one time.

*A few years back, I contacted Charlotte Reid, Reverend Reid's daughter, and asked her about Charlie Smith's grave. She was not familiar with the Charlie-Smith story, nor did she think there was a tombstone in the cemetery with his name on it. I may have found his family in the census living in Marumsco. It was a family that had a daughter with several young children living with her parents. Just maybe, Grandpop George adopted one of the children to take some of the burden off the family.

George had a sister named Hope who may have been Roger Swift's mother. Dad said there was some hanky panky somewhere in the Matthews and Swift families which may explain where Charlie came from. Those were not his exact words, but we will leave it there.

Grandpop George was of the Presbyterian faith and converted to the Baptist Church. At the age of seventy-eight he had a tumor removed from his hip at McCready Hospital in Crisfield, MD. The tumor weighed three-and-a-half pounds. Dr. George Coulbourne did the surgery, and George would not let the doctor put him to sleep for the operation. He remained active until about five days before his death and died of prostate cancer. George died June 15, 1943 at the age of ninety-three and is buried at Rehobeth Baptist Church.

Grandmom Jo—as Daddy called her—was born September 28, 1860. She was a tall slender woman with dark hair and known to be a very kind and loving person (photograph). She was a fabulous cook who loved to grow flowers. She spent her time working in the garden, canning the crops, and drying fruits on a roof top. Josephine and George had four children and two of them were stillborn. They had a daughter named Addie and a son named Grover. Addie only lived to be four or five years old, and Dad believed that she had died from pneumonia. (photograph). Her tombstone states she was born in 1861, but all records dispute that.

Grover A Matthews and sister Ada Florence Matthews.
She died at about age five years of pneumonia.
Photo 1900

Coventry Parish Birth Records, Rehobeth, MD
Ada Florence Matthews, female born 25 July 1885.
Christening Date: 28 July 1886
Age: 1 year. Christened at Coventry Parish, Rehobeth, MD
Father: George A Matthews
Mother: Josephine Matthews
Film # 14417

Grandmom Jo raised Dad from the time he was seven years old and died from stomach cancer when he was seventeen. She did not live to see him graduate from high school, passing away on Valentine's Day, February 14, 1934.

Aunt Josie said that Daddy failed his class the year his grandmother died, but he went back and repeated it, so he could graduate the next year. He did not mention that in our conversations.

I called the board of education in Somerset County a few years back inquiring about yearbooks or pictures of graduating classes in the 1930s.

They thought I was off my rocker.

My great-great-grandfather was Henry Matthews, but I don't know when he was born or when he died. Henry lived to be ninety-eight years old, at which time he was killed by an ox cart hauling lumber. The ox threw him against a tree and the cart wheels pinned him. No one found him until after he had died. Henry Matthews married Charity Swift.

I don't know when my great-great-grandmother, Charity Swift Matthews was born or when she died, but she lived to be 102 years old.

This was the end of Daddy's knowledge about the family, and let the records show that he was correct about ninety percent of the time with the birth, death, and marriage dates, all off the top of his head. How many can lay claim to such a great memory?

So, where do we go from here?

I still have two questions, and I doubt I will ever know the answers.

Number 1: Where did Amy G. Marshall meet Grover A. Matthews?

Number 2: Who is buried in the old graveyard on the Matthews property, and what was written on that tombstone? Rereading Daddy's notes he said a sibling was buried on the Matthews property. Is it safe to assume that was baby George? Maybe so.

I never heard Daddy degrading his father, other than to speak of those two beatings. He never complained about the strict way he was raised, but little peeks into his childhood popped up here and there. Such was the case in a letter that his grandmother Jo wrote and mailed to Mom-Mom Amy and Aunt Josie in July of 1932. Aunt Josie had the letter and sent me a copy. Daddy was not quite sixteen at the time and working in the fields.

Marion Stama
July 29 1932

Dear Sister
    & Mother
                I will now
write you a line in
answer to the one I
received from you some
time ago Lake would
of written but he is kept
busy out in the field
he did start to write once
and the mail left him
I am lots better now
am up going around
but of curse I dont
do much work and
as soon as I get a
chance I am coming

to see you hope you are
all well Lake Says
tell his Grandpa to
not forget his bucket
of figs and he will
be down some Saturday
after them guess I will
close now Lovingly
    from
        GrandMother
        & Lake

ON THE ROAD TO FROG EYE

PART II

Marumsco

The meaning of the word "Marumsco," comes from the Algonquian Indians: "where there are stones, of some kind."

Matthews is a patronymic surname meaning basically "son of Matthew." The given name Matthew, from which it is derived, means "gift of Yahweh" or "gift of God," from the Hebrew personal name Matityahu. Mathis is the German version of the surname. Matthews with a double "t" was more popular in Wales. Alternate spellings of the surname include Mathew, Matthew, Matthew, Mathis, Matheu (Old French) Mateo (Spanish) Matteo (Italian) and Mateus (Portuguese).

So, who were these ancestors that insisted the last name be written with two "t"s? For the most part, large families in the Matthews clan were not the norm compared with other families of the time. So, the memories and the stories had run out, but the history was buried somewhere, and it was time to dig.

I finally got deep into genealogy research in 2007, two years after Mother's death. I had been dabbling a little into the Joneses, and Aunt Thalia was teaching me the ropes. In fact, it was she who got me into this never-ending journey, but it is much easier than dealing with the living. I could not find any information on a Henry Matthews from Somerset County, nor could I locate a Charity Swift who fit into the projected time frame. I must have played with Matthews history for two years at least.

The names that Daddy had given me were not to be located. I hit a brick wall that I could not break through and did not understand why. I found plenty of Matthews but no Henry. Aunt Josie told me that Grandpop George and his two brothers, Robert and Ambrose, had bought adjoining farms in the Marumsco/Rehobeth area. She also knew that Ambrose had married Laura Darby, sister to our great-grandmother, Josephine Darby, making the children double cousins.

It was not until 2012 that I met another researcher, Bob Purnell, from Somerset County on Ancestry.com. His great uncle, George Purnell, had married Betty Hoffman, the sister of Carl Hoffman, Sr, and Carl was married to our Aunt Agnes. He contacted me regarding information on the Hoffmans. Weeks later, during one of our conversations, I told him about my brick wall. He had access to the old *Crisfield Times* and was able to pull newspaper articles including obituaries. I have never gone back searching for more information.

The Crisfield Times
Friday, February 16, 1934

Marion Resident Claimed By Death: *Mrs. Josephine Matthews died Wednesday night at the age of 73, from infirmities of age at her late home near Marion on last Wednesday night, after a lingering illness.*

Mrs. Matthews was a woman of lovable disposition and was a devout Christian. She was well known in Somerset County and had quite a wide circle of friends and acquaintances. Her many friends will mourn her loss. She is survived by her husband, Mr. George Matthews, one son, Mr. Grover Matthews and two sisters, Mrs. William Daugherty of Crisfield and Mrs. Ambrose Matthews of Rehobeth.

Funeral services will be held from her late home tomorrow (Saturday) afternoon at 2:30 pm, conducted by Rev. Harold Fordhain, assisted by Rev. Proyer of Rehobeth Baptist Church. Interment will be made in the Baptist Cemetery at Rehobeth.

I found it strange that Daddy was not named in his grandmother's obituary. I did locate a copy of Josephine Darby Matthews' will on the Mormon website.

The Crisfield Times
Friday, May 27th, 1938

Ambrose Matthews To Be Buried Today

Ambrose Matthews, prominent resident of Rehobeth, died Wednesday at his home in that community following an illness of two years. His wife, Mrs. Laura Virginia Matthews passed away in August 1934. He was born seventy two years ago in Fairmount and was the son of Robert H. Matthews and Charity Ballard Matthews of Fairmount.

Before ill health overtook him, the deceased was well known and a successful farmer who daily went about his labors in his usual industrious manner.

Though ill for many years, Mr. Matthews kept his usual cheerful way and greeted his many friends who called on him with his beaming smile.

Surviving are two daughters, Mrs. Annie Thompson of Rehobeth and Mrs. Roland Pennington of Baltimore; three grandchildren, Mrs. Clarence Tyler, Virginia Lee Pennington of Baltimore and Winfield Thompson of Rehobeth. Two brothers, Mr. George Matthews and Mr. Robert Matthews of Rehobeth also survive.

Funeral services will be held from his late home at 6 o'clock this evening with the Rev. Elmer Pryor, pastor of the Rehobeth Baptist Church officiating. Interment will be in Parkwood cemetery, Baltimore, Saturday.

The Crisfield Times
Friday, June 18, 1943
Aged Farmer Died At Rehobeth

George Matthews
Father of Grover Matthews the
grandfather of Lake S. Matthews and
Josephine M. Matthews

George Alfred Matthews Has Passed His 93rd Birthday

Funeral Was Held At Rehobeth On Thursday for George Alfred Matthews, one of the best known and highly respected farmers of the Rehobeth section died at his home there Tuesday morning of the infirmities of his age.

Outliving all other members of his family, he was 93 years and one month old. He came from a long lived family, most of whom reached very advanced ages before death claimed them. For the past 43 years he had lived on the farm where he died on Tuesday, and for most of that time was active in carrying on farming operations.

He was the son of the late Henry Matthews and Charity Bozman Matthews, prominent Somerset county residents, His wife, Mrs. Josephine Matthews died in 1934.

Funeral services were held yesterday, Thursday at the Rehobeth Baptist Church with the pastor, Rev. James McClode, officiating. Burial was beside the body of his wife in the churchyard. Pall bearers were Wallace Briddell, Roy Briddell, Rome Adams, Allen Adams, Joshua Adams and Emory Payne.

Surviving him are an only son, Grover Matthews, who lives at Rehobeth, two grandchildren, Lake Matthews who lives with his father and Mrs. Millard Daugherty of Crisfield, and one great grandchild, Millard Kirk Daugherty, the infant son of his grandaughter. A number of nephews and nieces, among the leading citizens of the county, also survive.

Register of Deeds, Somerset County, MD

On my last trip to the courthouse, I located a deed dated March 26, 1907 from George A. Matthews to Josephine Matthews:

In the consideration of seven-hundred dollars, I the said George A. Matthews, do grant and hereby convey unto Josephine Matthews of said county and state all that lot or parcel of land situated in Brinkleys Election District in Somerset County, Maryland and on the east side of the county road known as the "Marumsco County Road" and adjoining a tract of land called "Kings Hat" and "Adams Garden" and being part of the homestead of Calvin A. McCready, deceased, and containing 30 acres more or less, and being this same land which was conveyed to me the said George A. Matthews by Edward Broughton and Samuel Broughton by deed dated on the first day of August in the year nineteen hundred and one and recorded among the land records of somerset County in Libre QTA no, 35 Folio 183.

My guess is this would be when he had the large tumor removed that Daddy spoke about and transferred the property to Josephine before surgery in case he did not survive.

Josephine Darby Matthews had another sister named Florence, and obviously she picked up her sister's name when she named their daughter Ada Florence. I did a little research on her sister and found she was born in 1866 in Shelltown, so she was a few years younger than Josephine. She married William D. Daugherty of Crisfield in 1892. Their second son was named Lake Conway Daugherty, and Aunt Josie said she thought the name Lake came from a minister on Smith Island, but she wasn't sure. It seems logical that Daddy was named after Grover's first cousin, Lake Conway, but there's no way to confirm it. Lake Conway Daugherty was a brakeman for the railroad and lived in Crisfield. He was killed by a freight train on December 30, 1940 at the age of forty-four. His death certificate states that he was run over by a freight train and crushed. The accident happened in Deep Creek, Virginia, Princess Anne County. One year and one day later Florence (our great-aunt) died on December 31, 1941 at the age of seventy-three.

Second Great-Grandparents:

We now know that Henry Matthews' legal name was Robert Henry Matthews. I located Ambrose Matthews' death certificate that had been filled out by his daughter, Annie Thompson, and she stated that Ambrose's mother was Charity Ballard, but in George Matthews' obituary it states that his mother was Charity Bozman, which led to more questions. Looking back now, I know there was a family Bible at the Matthews home, and Grover would have been the one to fill out his father's death certificate, so was it possible that he pulled Charity's name from the family Bible? Did George and Ambrose have different mothers, as Charity was a common name at the time.

While scrolling through the old census records searching for Bozmans and Ballards in the area, I stumbled on a gentleman by the name of Ballard Bozman, and the bells went off. I assume that cousin Annie had heard the name Ballard and must have gotten confused with the given name and the surname, but it had to be proven. When I learned that George's brother Robert B. Matthews' middle initial stood for Bozman, I knew the correct maiden name for our second great-grandmother, was Charity Bozman.

1850 Federal Census:
Henry Matthews, age 30 and wife Charity, age 28. They have 4 daughters: Mary, age 10, Sarah, age 7, Susan, age 6 and Martha, age 2.

1860 Federal Census:
Henry born in 1819 and the Post Office is listed as Rehobeth. Henry, age 40, Charity, age 45, Mary, age 19, Sarah, age 17, Susan, age 15, Martha, age 12; Robert, age 10, Amanda, age 6; George, age 5, Ambrose, age 2.
They had 4 children in the ten-year span since the last census and ware living nextdoor to Robert Henry's parents.

1870 Federal Census:
Henry, age 52, farmer, Charity age 52, keeping house, George age 12, attending school, Ambrose, age 10, attending school. Value of personal estate is $300. Neither Henry nor Charity can read or write. Also living in the household are Henry Ennis, age 26 a farm laborer. His wife, Martha is 22 and keeping house. (This would be their daughter Martha and husband). There is also Isaac Duer living there. He is a huckster and has real estate valued at $1000 and personal property worth $200. The post office is listed as Princess Anne, MD.

1880 Federal Census:
Henry is a farmer, age 66, and this time the census shows him born in 1814. Charity is now 65 and all three sons are living at home. George is single, 23 years old, and a farm laborer; Ambrose is single and is 22 years old. Robert B., the oldest son is now married, a farm laborer and 28 years old. His wife Lizzie is 24 and they have two boys. Milton age 4, and Isaac H. Matthews, 9 months old. George is the only one in the household who can read or write. They are living in Brinkley's District in Somerset County, MD

January15, 1839:
Court records show Henry Matthews married Sarah Melvin in Somerset County. MD

January 25, 1840:
Court records show Henry Matthews married Charity Ann Bozman in Worchester County, Md, on the Maryland-Virginia Line.

March 1840:
Court records show that Henry Matthews divorced Sarah Melvin. (probably when it was recorded) Research was done by Lloyd Matthews and is resourced and recorded.

November 25, 1892:

Charity Matthews, a widow, files for military pension of Robert H. Matthews who served with K1E.S. Infantry in Maryland. Application #56H55. Research shows that Henry served in the infantry regiment that was formed in Cambridge to protect the homefront, and I was surprised to read it fell under the command of the Union. At some point the regiment was ordered to report to Gettysburg, but they refused to go, as it was in their agreement. Consequently, most, if not all, of those who served were denied a pension. I have a newspaper article regarding the fight and research done by R. Purnell, the same person who sent me the obituaries. We do not know if Charity was approved or denied the pension after his death.

The National Archives:

Detail-Matthew, Robert H...Organization Index to Pension Files of Veterans who served between 1861 and 1900. *I have not ordered the records for him, as we have the index card, but it is available at the archives should anyone care to pay for the research. The last time I checked the charge was $75.00 and that was years ago.

1900 Federal Census, taken June 1:

There is no census for 1890 as those records were destroyed by fire many years ago, so we do not know in which part of the county the family was living and cannot pin down Robert Henry's death, other than before 1892. In 1900 we find Charity Matthews, a widow, living with her son, George. She states that she was born in 1805 and is 94 years old when the census was taken two months before her 95th birthday. Charity states that she has had 11 children and that 7 are living. She does not read or write, but does speak English. George is age 44, born in February 1856. Josephine is 39, born March 1861. She had 4 children and one is living, including our grandfather Grover, age 11 and attending school. George, Josephine, and Grover can all read and write. Charlie Smith, a Black servant lives there. He is 19 years old, and cannot read or write but does speak English.

By the 1910 census, Charity was no longer living in the Matthews household. I have never been able to locate the graves of our paternal second great-grandparents, Henry and Charity, but since George's obituary states he was born in Fairmont in Somerset County, I have a feeling they are buried there.

So, did Daddy get it right when he said that Charity lived to be 102 years old? If so, that means she passed away in 1907, and since I have only found maybe one death that he might have been off on, I ran with it and listed her to have reached that grand old age of 102. Everybody on Ancestry.com has copied 1907 as her death date.

Ambrose and Laura had two daughters, Pearl and Annie (Cousin Annie). Pearl married a Pennington and lived in Baltimore. It is their child that is buried in the Matthews plot at Rehobeth Baptist Church. It took me years to figure out who the child was. Either Mother or Aunt Josie had told me that the child was connected to Cousin Annie, but they did not know how. Cousin Annie married Alfred Thompson (the one who looked like a Quaker) and they had one son, Winfield, who became the surgeon.

Robert Bozman Matthews, their older brother, married Sarah Elizabeth Foster and they had seven children, according to the 1900 census: Robert B, age 49; Sarah E, age 45, Milton, age 25, Henry, age 20, Ambrose, age 18, Foster, age 13, Elonzo, age 11, and Addie, age 4 (the Cousin Addie that I remember).

One of Henry and Charity's daughters, Amanda Hope Matthews, married a Theophilus Swift, and had son named Roger Swift. The same Mr. Roger whose hair I combed every night by the old woodstove and the Mr. Roger that hauled me in that horse and buggy to gather the potatoes or on a hayride back to the barn. He was my grandfather's first cousin who treated us like his grandchildren. Mr. Roger had a sister named Charity Swift after her grandmother and that is where Daddy got confused with Charity's last name.

I have not researched the other children of Henry and Charity and it appears that Robert "Henry" died at age seventy-three and did not live as long as Daddy remembered. Most records indicate that Robert Henry was born c.1819. He may have gotten that confused with the age of George A. Matthews.

Our third great-grandparents were Whittington Matthews and Sarah Muir. It appears that Whittington was born about 1790 and Sarah about 1792. They married on February 15, 1820, (documented in public records) a year after Henry was born, so was Sarah his mother? I do not know the answer.

1850 Federal Census:
Whittington is a farmer, age sixty, and has a real estate value of $1000. Wife Sarah is age fifty-eight and there are two children living in the household. Sarah Jr, age 16 and William, age 15. They cannot read or write, and they live nextdoor to Henry and Charity.

1860 Federal Census:
Whittington, age sixty and wife Sally, age fifty with a child by the name of Martha Williams, age 14 living with them. They still live nextdoor to Henry and Charity. I have read that their daughter Sarah married a Williams, so this may have been a granddaughter. Whittington was 70 and his wife just a little younger at this time. I do not find them in the 1870 census, so I assume that Whittington is deceased and she had moved. I have listed his death as before 1870 and as you see the census taker could not add. This was too common in the old records, but at least he could write.

The first federal census was not until 1790, so now we are out of stories that were either passed down or from the census. There is no will recorded for Whittington Matthews in Somerset County, MD. The remainder will have to come from court records. Many of the name orders were done by a researcher by the name of Ruth Dryden on the older ancestors and forwarded to me by Lloyd Matthews, also a descendant of the Matthews. All are well-documented, and some can be found online, as well as my years of searching on Ancestry.com, the Mormon records, and a couple trips to the courthouse in Princess Anne, MD searching for documents to prove the lineage.

Our Fourth Great-Grandparents

Levi Matthews was born 26 March, 1773 at Conventry Parish in Rehobeth (Somerset County). He was married at least twice, and I do not know in which order. He was married to Priscilla unknown. I just acquired an old map from Ronald Adams dated 1870 of Marumsco, and it shows several families by the last name Whittington living close to the Matthews families on the western side of Marumsco Creek, so my hunch is she may have been a Whittington. Their son, Whittington, is the only male that I have found by that name in the family, so I feel fairly confident it was Priscilla's maiden name.

On April 3, 1811 he married Nancy Dickerson in Somerset County. Consequently, I cannot confirm which is our fourth great-grandmother, but if Priscilla was a Whittington, we have our answer. More research is needed.

SOMERSET COUNTY LAND RECORDS

February 16, 1796: Denwood Matthews to Levi Matthews for "Knights Success," devised to grantor William Matthews. Recorded Book K, Page 324-325

February 5, 1799: Bill of sale, Levi Matthews to Esme Merrill for negro, Henry on Jan 1, 1799. Recorded Book L, Page 391

Register Of Wills, Princess Anne Courthouse, Somerset County, MD Dated March 5, 1829.

Levi Matthews filed a strange will in Somerset County, and it is difficult to understand.

I Levi Matthews of Somerset County, State of Maryland do make this my last will and testament. Item: I give and bequeath unto James Bloyd one cow and calf. Item: I give and bequeath unto Mary Bloyd a home where I now live as long as she lives single also I give unto her a cow and calf, one feather bed and furniture and a sow and four shoats. Item: I give and bequeath unto my wife all my lands and tenements during her life, also all the ____of my personal property after my debts are paid. Item: I give and bequeath all my lands after the death of my wife unto William and Whittington Matthews, to them and their heirs forever on condition that the said William and Whittington Matthews shall within three months after my death give up unto my executor the notes that I have given them. Should they or either of them refuse or neglect to do the service then I give and bequeath the said lands *unto John Williams of Worchester County, MD on condition that he shall pay William and Whittington any amount that I am indebted to them, but should he refuse I do inform my executor to sell in the manner that he thinks best. I do appoint James Stewart* Executor... *March 5th, 1829*

I have no clue who James and Mary Bloyd were unless maybe step-children or a niece and nephew. I copied the will when I went to the courthouse. Levi sounds like he had an attitude when it came to his two sons.

Fifth Great-Grandparents:

David Matthews was born in 1741 in Conventry Parish, Somerset County. We find in the old Conventry Parish Marriage Records that David Matthews married Sarah Carsley or Cearsley in 1767.

I, David Matthews being rendered by old age weak and infirm of body but of sound and perfect mind and memory and willing to settle my estate do make this my last will and testament viz; Item: I give and bequeath all my lands where I now live and give all of my marshes unto my son Edward Matthews to him and his heirs forever. Item: I give unto my dear and loving wife Sarah Matthews all of my flax, cotton and wool & bed & furniture. One cow and calf to her and her heirs forever. Item: I leave unto my son Edward Matthews one cow and calf and my negro boy named Harry to him and his heirs forever. I likewise leave unto Edward one bed and furniture. Item: I leave unto my daughter Betsy Matthews one negro girl named Juday and one bed and furniture, one cow and calf. I leave unto Edward Matthews my ox cart and one yoke of oxen. I leave unto my wife Sarah Matthews one yoke of oxen and likewise leave unto my wife two ewes. I give unto Edward Matthews two ewes. I give to my wife Sarah my riding mare. I leave my crop that's now on hand to my wife Sarah Matthews and my son Edward Matthews and my daughter Betsy Matthews to them to support for the term of next year. Item: My will and desire is that if Edward shall die without heirs, that my son Israel Matthews shall inherit my lands. If Israel shall die without heirs my son Joshua shall become next to enjoy my lands. Item: I leave the remaining part of my property not before given away to be equally divided between my children and wife. That is to say Sarah Matthews and Elijah, Casey, Levi Matthews, Israel Matthews, Joshua Matthews, Edward and Betsy Matthews to them and their heirs forever. Last of all I do constitute and appoint my wife Sarah Matthews my Executor of this my last will and testament and witness my hand and seal this thirteenth day of November, Seventeen Hundred and Ninety Six. (1796) David Matthews, his mark.

I copied this will when I went to the courthouse in Princess Anne. It was customary at that time for the oldest son to inherit the majority of the land and personal property as women were not allowed to own property. This is the first mention of owning slaves that I have seen in our straight lineage but many were owned by some of the Matthews families. Levi must have owned at least one also, as he sold a Negro named Henry in 1799.

Sixth Great-Grandparents:
Teague Matthews born 1695 in Somerset County, Maryland married Elizabeth Adams born 1710 in Somerset County, MD

Maryland Early Census:
Date 1723
Teague Matthews: Township, Pocomoke 100 in Somerset County, MD

Maryland Early Census:
Date 1745
Teague Matthews: Township, Coventry Parish (Rehobeth, MD)

Register of Wills, Somerset County Courthouse/Princess Anne, Maryland. Dated November 23, 1760.

In the name of God Amen the twenty third day of November in the year of our Lord God 1760, I Teague Matthews of Somerset County in the province of Maryland, Planter being very unfirm in body but of perfect mind and memory Thanks be given to God therefore calling to mind the mortality of my body and knowing that it is appointed for all men to die do make and ordain this my Last Will and Testament. That is to say ____and first of all I give and recommend my soul into the hands of God that gave it and for my body ____it to the earth to be buried in a Christian like and decent manner at the discretion of my executor. It is my will and I do order that in the first place all of my just debts be paid and satisfied.

Item: I give and bequeath unto my grandson Benjamin Holland Matthews one hundred acres of land called "Worthless" to the said Benjamin and his heirs. (Bottom line got cut off)

Item: A tract of land to my dutiful son David Williams and to the heirs lawfully begotten of his body; and likewise I do order and it is my last will that my son David Matthews should have the benefit of the said plantation and to keep it in good repairs and plant an orchard on the same and keep it clear of all manner of incumbrances until the said Benjamin arrives to the age of twenty one years and in consideration thereof I do order that when Benjamin receives the said land and plantation with the appurtenances those belonging to give a receipt to my executor for thirty four pounds which becomes his right of his deceased father Philip Matthews, Estate. Likewise, I give and bequeath unto my grandson Benjamin Holland Matthews half the marsh which I hold on the western most side of the mouth of Marumsco Creek called the "Haphazzard" to him and his heirs lawfully begotten by his body, and if he departs this life without lawful issue to descend as the above said plantation.

Item: I give and bequeath to my dutiful son David Matthews all the remaining part of my lands and marshes which I hold after my well beloved wife Elizabeth's widowhood to him the said David and to the heirs lawfully begotten by his body. But if my son David should depart this life without lawful heirs it is to descend to my two daughters

Tabitha Matthews and Betty Matthews and to be equally divided among them and their lawful heirs after my beloved wife's widowhood and for my beloved wife not to be debarred of any benefits of the said land and marshes during her widowhood. She is to keep it clear of all manner of incumbrances.

Item: I give and bequeath unto my dutiful daughter Tabitha Matthews one cow and calf and one feather bed and furniture and two pewter dishes and six pewter plates.

Item: I give and bequeath unto my dutiful daughter Betty Matthews one cow and calf and one feather bed and furniture and two pewter dishes and six pewter plates.

Item: I leave unto my well loved wife Elizabeth all the remaining part of my personal estate and what is _____in her maintenance and raising my children after her widowhood, I give and bequeath unto my four daughters Viz; Sarah, Rebekah, Tabatha and Betty to be equally divided amongst them.

Item: I appoint, constitute, make and ordain my son David Matthews my only and sole executor of this my last will and testament and I do hereby utterly disallow revoke and dismiss all and every other former will and testaments. In witness whereof I have ___unto set my hand then affixed my seal the day and year written above is signed, sealed and pronounced and declared by the said Teague Matthews as his last will and testament in the presence of Teague Riggin, John Matthews, John Riggin and Samuel Adams. Signed by Teague Matthews mark.

Copied at the courthouse in Princess Anne, MD. Phillip appears to have been the oldest son of Teague. Therefore his son Benjamin Holland Matthews was to inherit most of the Teague's estate on his 21st birthday. Records show that his widow Elizabeth Adams died in 1765.

THE BASTARD BOY

Seventh Great-Grandfather: William Matthews

Maryland Marriages 1634-1777

William Matthews married Mary Riggin at Somersetshire, Maryland in 1688. Mary was born the 4th of January 1668, the daughter of Teague Riggin and Mary London. Teague Riggin was from Ireland and in his will dated 1707, he left twelve pence in silver to his son in law, William Matthews.

Somerset County Birth Records

William Matthews son of Wm. Matthews born of Mary his wife ye 11th June One thousand six hundred eighty four.
Entered October 28th 1682:
Mary Matthews (onet) daughter of Wm. Matthews and born of Mary his wife the fourth day of November and Domini one thousand six hundred eighty six
ut supra – Ellis Mathews daughter of William Mathews was born the ninth day of January anno one thousand six hundred eighty eight.
Note that the clerk used one "t" for Mathews in these records.

Somerset County Judicial Records 1689-1690

Teague Riggin beats wife Mary Riggin with an 18-inch board. Volume 106, Page 188 Teague Riggin and Mary would be our eighth great-grandparents, and it seems he had a bit of that hot Irish temper in his genes.

This is the last will that I transcribed, and it is an important one, as it gives us a glimpse into the life our seventh great-grandfather, William

Matthews, born June 9, 1661 in Hungars Parish, Northampton, Virginia. William's birth recorded in Virginia, U.S. Extracted Vital Records 1660-1923.

It is clear that William was a devout Christian, grateful for his blessings and loved his wife and family without question.

Maryland Register of Wills, Annapolis, Maryland

In the name of God Amen, I William Matthews of Somerset County in Maryland being sick & weak of body but perfect of mind and memory provided be God for it & calling to mind the uncertainty of all things here on earth that all men must submit to death when it shall please God to call them, I do make this & ordain this my last will and testament in manner & form following (viz) First I give and bequeath my soul to God my maker _____ through the _____ death of Jesus Christ my savior to receive free & full pardon & forgiveness of all my sins & my body I give to the earth from whence I was taken be buried at the discretion of my friends, in Christian burial & as for my Temporal Estate wherewith it has phased God to bless me with, I give & bequeath as followeth:

Item: I give and bequeath to my eldest son William Matthews part of a tract of land called "Edwin" beginning at the first boundaries running & binding upon the creek hole little slash of marsh & running by a piece of ground called the "Mill" on the eastern most side of the mill, likewise that the tract of land called "Elliott" all that part of the eastern most side, binding on the creek. Likewise I give unto my son William for dividing a tract of land called "Edwin" part of this said land running from the slash into the woods to the eastern most side of the pond____ wing in a slash of marsh & for length of his and running into the woods to a Gumm thicket standing by the main road and for ____with a straight course to the split bridge & from thence to the first bound for him the said William to live upon where he now lives & to clear ground & get timber for his self & likewise have the benefit of young orchard which he planted & now have the benefit of my well beloved wife Mary not to be debarred on the manner plantation where I now live.

Item: I give & bequeath unto my son John Matthews and my son William fifty acres of marsh called "Meadows" beginning at the mouth of Hillards/ Killards Gut. One to have as much privilege as the other not debarring my well beloved wife Mary of any privilege shall think to make for her own during her widowhood.

Item: I give unto my sons Teague & Samuel that parcel of marsh the "Hook" last is to say from the beginning to a sedar stake sett down in the said marsh near the division fence. My well beloved wife Mary not to be debarred of the benefit during her widowhood. The marsh I give & bequeath unto my sons Teague & Samuel & to their heirs forever.

Item: I give & bequeath unto Jacob Adams to him & his heirs forever a part of that parcel of marsh last mentioned, that is to say from the sedar stake northward & westward to the creek.

Item: I give & bequeath to my son David Matthews a tract of land in the woods called "Worthless" by estimation one hundred & ten acres to him and his heirs forever.

Item: I give unto my daughter Sarah Matthews one feather bed & furniture, three pewter dishes, three plates & one basin & 10 cattle, their increase now is called hers & one good iron pot.

Item: I give to my son Samuel one featherbed and furniture.

Item: I give & bequeath unto my four youngest children (viz) David; Elizabeth; Rachell; & Martha all the rest & remainder part of my personal Estate what so ever, my debts being paid & funeral expenses discharged. My dear & loving wife not to be disbarred of any part or parcel there of during her widowhood or natural life and after her decease to be equally divided among the four above said "Viz" David; Elizabeth; Rachell; & Martha.

Lastly, I do appoint & ordain my well beloved wife Mary to be my sole executor of this my last will and testament hereby revoking all former wills what so ever by me made. Hereby declaring for willingness to himself I have here unto set my hand & fixed my seal this fourth day of October in the year of our Lord Anno D 1726.

William "M" Matthews his mark

In the presense of

Jacob Adams

Robert Taylor

Thomas Maddox

So, it seems that our seventh great-grandfather, labeled *The Bastard Boy*, turned out to be a great gentleman, husband, and father.

Eighth Great-Grandmother: Elice Nebulian

Our seventh great-grandfather, William Matthews was the son of Morice Matthews and Elice Nebulian and born out of wedlock on June 9, 1661 in Northampton County, VA. His mother Elice was an orphaned Irish servant at age fifteen or sixteen when he was born. Morice was the son of an Englishman and had come to America in 1651 according to documentation. Documentation does not specify rape, but I would bet my soul that it was nothing other. At one time, there was a copy of the reference book page from Northampton County, VA courthouse online and they referenced William as "The Bastard Boy" in the old book. The book can probably be located in the courthouse or library in Northampton County, VA.

On July 3, 1661, exactly fifty-two days after the birth of William, his mother Elice Nebulian married another Irish servant by the name of Donnack Dennis. Donnack Dennis was born in 1645 in Ireland. There are some notations on ancestry that Donnack too was an orphan. Shortly after their marriage Dennis moved to Somerset County with his wife and her son, William Matthews.

Maryland Early Census shows Donnack registered for a cattle mark in the year 1667 in Somerset County, MD.

Documented in "Old Somerset on the Eastern Shore of Maryland, a study in foundation and founders," Donnack and Elice had five children: Elizabeth, born November 16, 1665, Margaret, born February 8, 1667, Donnack, born February 16, 1668, Ellis, born July 29, 1673, and John born in 1676. Some records indicate that our eighth great-grandmother, Elice Neubulian, died around 1687 in Somerset County and that Donnack remarried. The records are a bit confusing and difficult to translate.

Donnack's will is dated 16 February and probated on 23 March, 1717. He leaves three-hundred acres to his wife, but does not name her. He leaves numerous tracks of land, tobacco, and silver to his grandchildren. He does not mention William, but there are numerous writings indicating that Donnack treated William as his own son. He registered a cattle mark for William in Somerset County early on.

Donnack is listed as an early settler of Somerset County in the records "They Settled in Somerset." He was well known and obviously respected. and held many government positions with the higher courts.

THE REAL BASTARD

Passenger & Immigration List Index, 1500 -1900

Name: Morice Matthews

Arrival Year: 1651

Arrival Place: Virginia

Primary Immigrant: Mathews, Morice

Source: Publication Code: 2772

Early Virginia Immigrants, 1623-1666

Mathews, Morice, 1653, sponsored by Edward Harrington N. H. County

He may have sailed back to England and returned again to Virginia.

Virginia, US Extracted Vital Records, 1660-1923

William Matthews ye sonne of Morice Matthews and Elise Nebulian born June 9th.

Register of Wills, Dorchester County, Md, British America

Morice Matthews registered his will on the 3rd of September 1705 in Dorchester County, MD. It was probated on 28th of April 1707.

To Elinor daughter of Edward Wright, 60 acres

To: Sarah Pennington & John Vincent, the personal belongings of my estate.

To: Ishmail Riding, 2 years of his service and time.

To: John and Thomas, sons of Hugh Eccleston, 100 acres known as "Daniel's Pasture,"

100 acres known as "Newton's Desire," 100 acres known as "Hodcans Point," also a tract of land obtained from Arthur Wright in July 1695.

The will is filed at Annapolis, Maryland Land Office...Will Book 12 Page 298

Morice's will leaves all his properties and personal belongings to neighbors or friends. I have never located records that he married. So, William, the son of Morice was not mentioned in his father's will. For all we know, William did not acknowledge him as his father, but called Donnack father and no doubt the only one that he had ever known.

Note: We have over 370 years of Matthews documented in America and all except one owning land in Somerset County since the mid 1600s. I asked and got an answer from Mary Jo today that Allen Matthews owns about five acres of the original Matthews farm. Allen is the last Matthews to live in Marumsco and still on *The Road to Frog Eye* even if they do call it Cornstalk Road these days.

There are no males in our direct lineage to carry the Matthews name forward, as Wayne has two daughters, Allen has one daughter, and Glen never married nor had children. Ambrose Matthews' name died out years ago, as he had two daughters. I am in touch with a cousin Sandy Matthews Marshall, a descendant of Robert Bozman Matthews, and as of today, she confirmed that there are two males in that lineage, grandsons of Ronnie Matthews, her brother. There are males in other lines that are still living as they too have done Matthews research and there are lots of cousins that popped up in the DNA matches. It appears that we would have to go back five generations to find other male descendants.

MATTHEWS DEATH RECORDS

Lake S. Matthews.................... died April 11, 1987 at age 70

Margaret Jones Matthews............died August 17, 2005 at age 83 (2 months shy of 84th birthday)

Glen Ingram Matthews................died August 18, 2010 at age 57 (son of Margaret & Lake)

Josephine M. Matthews Daugherty..died December 26, 2015 at age 91 (6 weeks shy of age 92nd birthday)

Millard Kirk Daughtery................died December 26, 2017 at age 75 (son of Josephine & Millard Daugherty)

Grover Allen Matthews................died October 14, 1963 at age 75

Amy Marshall Matthews..............died April 15, 1975 at age 84

Edna Jones Matthews.................died Sept 29, 1991 at age 81

George Alfred Matthews..............died June 15th at age 93

Josephine Darby Matthews..........died February 14 at age 72

Ada Florence Matthews...............died 1890(?) at age 5 (daughter of George and Josephine)

Robert Henry Matthews.............died before 1892 at age 72 or younger

Charity Bozman Matthews..........died about 1907 at age 92 or 102

Levi Matthews........................died in 1829 at age 56

Whittington Matthews...............died before 1870 between the ages of 70 and 80 years

David Matthews......................died in 1796 at age 55

Teague Matthews.....................died about 1790 at age 65

William Matthews....................died October 1726 at age 65

Elice Nebulian Dennis................died about 1687 at age 41

We know that Morice Matthews is recorded as arriving in America in 1651, the first of our Matthews forefathers to step into the New World. I care not to acknowledge his birth nor his death on the chart above.

I have only scratched the surface with the family history, and no doubt there is much to learn in the county clerk of deeds office. The Somerset County court records would be interesting, for sure. Maybe a member of the family reading this will carry on our journey. I have done my part.

Overall, our childhood was filled with pleasant memorable times and great adventures that many children do not get to experience. That said, it would take a child raised in the country to appreciate the stories, one where they too could reminisce. Like many, I was terrified of the storms from mother nature and the two-legged monster that kept returning to The Road to Frog Eye. It is clear that I was more terrified of being beaten by that leather belt, and my life may have taken a different path had I not been. I always told others that I wanted to be a "well-educated, traveling, goodwill ambassador," whatever that meant, and Mother would have helped me get there.

When Wayne and I followed Daddy through the marshlands near Marumsco Creek searching for that perfect cedar tree at Christmas, little did we know that our seventh great-grandfather William had pinned a "sedar" tree on that marsh. Not as a Christmas tree but to mark the boundaries of his land.

The day I got trapped in the center of the blackberry grove down near the creek by that stomping black bull, little did I know that our ancestors had planted orchards in the vicinity and more than likely it included berries.

All those Sunday afternoons that my barefooted friends and I spent crabbing with a chicken bone and string in the marshland of the creek, I never would have guessed that our ancestors and their children had probably crabbed and fished somewhere in those marshes 300 years before I ever got there.

Daddy did not know that our ancestors had lived in Marumsco more than 350 years, nor did he know that his first ancestor born in America was known as "The Bastard Boy," or he would have told me. Pop-Pop Grover and his father George more than likely did not know, or they would have told Daddy, and I seriously doubt Robert Henry knew, as he could neither read nor write. We will never know if William Matthews' story was passed down to his children and grandchildren or swept under the rug, but we now know.

I have read numerous times that we all really die twice—once when we take our last breath on this earth, and again when everyone forgets that we died. Do not let us die.

Indeed Daddy, you were right... *The road that leads to hell is paved with good intentions.*

JOYCE MATTHEWS MCQUEEN

September 10, 1943 – February 1, 2023

On Wednesday, February 1, 2023, Joyce Matthews McQueen, loving wife, mother, and grandmother passed away at age seventy-nine.

Joyce was a fierce and loving woman. In her early years she spent her time running old country roads and playing on farms or in creek beds with her siblings. In later years she spent her time as both a businesswoman and traveler. She took bus trips across the country for the heck of it, flew to different states in puddle jumper planes, and spent time with her friends and her children.

In her more recent years, she liked to spend her time in her flower beds, researching her ancestry, writing her books, and spending time with her friends and family.

Joyce was preceded in death by her father Lake Matthews, mother Margaret Matthews, and brother Glenn Matthews.

She is survived by her husband Johnnie McQueen; brother Wayne Matthews; sister Phyllis Jenkins; son Steve Thomas; daughters Terrie Stanbrook and Timley Shelton; grandsons Frankie Bushong, Tyler Bushong, Kyle Shelton, Chris Pack, Justin Stanbrook, and Mark Thomas; granddaughters Rachel Shelton, Bethany Roye, and Tiffany Thomas; nieces Jennifer Jenkins, Shannon Williams, and Chaily Herce, as well as many, many great-grandchildren, great-nieces, great-nephews, friends, and other loved ones.

Do not stand at my grave and weep
I am not there; I do not sleep.
I am a thousand winds that blow,
I am the diamond glints on snow.
I am the sun on ripened grain,
I am the gentle autumn rain.
When you awaken in the morning's hush,
I am the swift uplifting rush
Of quiet birds in circled flight.
I am the soft stars that shine at night.
Do not stand at my grave and cry,
I am not there; I did not die.

-Mary Elizabeth Frye

A celebration of life was held at Deltaville Maritime Museum on March 11, 2023 at 2:00pm.

Made in the USA
Middletown, DE
24 February 2023

25469340R00129